Caroline Sanderson is a writer whose work has appeared in *The Times*, *Mslexia* and *The Bookseller*, for whom she writes regular features on books and publishing, and a monthly column previewing new non-fiction titles. She is the author of the highly praised children's travel title *Pick Your Brains about Greece*, also published by Cadogan. Her ambition, in the words of Jane Austen, is to 'write only for fame, and without any view to pecuniary emolument.' She lives with her family in Gloucestershire.

A Rambling Fancy

A Rambling Fancy

in the footsteps of
Jane Austen

Caroline Sanderson

Published by Cadogan Guides 2006

Cadogan Guides
2nd Floor, 233 High Holborn
London WC1V 7DN
info@cadoganguides.co.uk
www.cadoganguides.com

The Globe Pequot Press
246 Goose Lane, PO Box 480, Guilford,
Connecticut 06437–0480

Typesetting by Mathew Lyons
Printed in Italy by Legoprint
A catalogue record for this book is available
from the British Library
ISBN 10: 1-86011-328-1
ISBN 13: 978-1-86011-328-4

Contents

You will think me rhapsodizing; but when I am out of doors, especially when I am sitting out of doors, I am very apt to get into this sort of wondering strain. One cannot fix one's eyes on the commonest natural production without finding food for a rambling fancy.

Fanny Price in *Mansfield Park* (Chapter 22)

Introduction
'Important nothings'

Where shall I begin? Which of all my important nothings shall I tell you first? – Letter to her sister Cassandra, 15 June 1808

There are already plenty of tourist guides to the places most associated with Jane Austen, and books of walks that will conduct you across towns and villages and fields while pointing out places she knew, as well as pubs that serve a decent lunch on the way. What I planned to do with this book was something rather different. I wanted to follow my nose and, like Fanny Price, get into a 'wondering strain' while sitting in pews or on stiles or in teashops, standing in fields or museums or churchyards. Then I would free-associate with the things I wrote down when re-reading her novels and letters, and ramble.

I have found one other book that attempts to do something similar, *Jane Austen: Her Homes and Her Friends*, first published in 1902. Its author, Constance Hill, journeyed around England with her sister Ellen. Hill adopts a reverential tone that can seem quaint to modern readers, but she had the advantage of walking in Jane Austen's footsteps less than 100 years after her death. England was still a relatively rural place and much less had changed then than in the century that separates Hill's time from ours. Hill was able to visit buildings still standing 100 years ago, such as the Assembly Rooms at Lyme Regis, that have since been demolished. Her journey was also more wide-ranging than mine, taking in the Abbey School at Reading, the County Ball-Room in Basingstoke, Southampton (where nothing remained of Jane's former home even in 1901) and Stoneleigh Abbey in Warwickshire, the home of Thomas Leigh, a relative of Jane's mother.

Charming as Constance Hill's book is, I felt that I could jus-tifiably revisit many of the same places and write about them as they are now, 200 years removed from Jane Austen's time. I made the decision not to try to provide a tourist guide and to restrict myself to places that could easily be visited by anyone with the interest to do so, with the one special exception of Godmersham Park, which is not open to the public but can be viewed at very close quarters from a public footpath. I solicited no insider knowledge, other than that which could be gleaned from books and tourist literature available to any visitor. As a result, my observations would largely be fresh and, however fan-ciful, my own.

Unlike Constance Hill, who undertook a much more com-prehensive pilgrimage, I decided to focus on places mentioned by Jane Austen in surviving letters, which record her impressions of them or, more often, of the people she knew in those places. I hoped that this would make it easier to compare then with now.

However, Jane Austen's letters are a famously incomplete source. For reasons she took to her own grave, her sister Cassandra destroyed the bulk of them after Jane's death, and her niece did for many others. Were they too rude, too emotional, too personal? According to Claire Tomalin, one of Jane Austen's recent biographers, 'Cassandra's culling, made for her own good reasons, leaves the impression that her sister was dedicated to trivia. The letters rattle on, sometimes almost like a comedian's patter. Not much feeling, warmth or sorrow has been allowed through.'[1] It's true that when reading them it's very difficult to take almost anything Jane writes seriously. What were the feelings that now go unexpressed? What grudges and quarrels, love affairs and crushes might have been consigned to the bonfire? It's agony to imagine. Imagine many have, even so. Jane Austen is perhaps the most written about of all English writers. A vast array of biographies and critical studies is available. Every facet of her life and work has been discussed, in the minutest of detail. Writers speculate and the books about Jane Austen accumulate. Yet, in the main, the woman herself still eludes us.

In his novel *Flaubert's Parrot* Julian Barnes likens the art of biography to fishing with a net. 'But think of everything that got away, that fled with the last deathbed exhalation of the biographee.'[2] Here I don't want to speculate too much about the things that got away. I want to focus on what remains to us of the flesh-and-blood Jane Austen: her work, of course, and her remaining letters, which, though full of large holes, are a joy and as essential a read for every devotee as *Pride and Prejudice*. I also want to focus on the places she knew. Some are lovingly preserved, welcoming thousands of visitors every year. Others are almost unknown, except to sheep or the most devoted of Jane Austen scholars. But each place has light to shed, in its own way.

Finally, I found inspiration in Fanny Price. Of all Jane Austen's heroines, she was the one I used not to get on with. I felt that she was far too good to be really interesting, a feeling I have shared with many other people. My husband, for instance, still shudders at the mention of her name 25 years after studying *Mansfield Park* at school. Yet, re-reading the novel, I realized that the whole point about mouse-like Fanny is that you would miss her if she wasn't there. You don't take much notice of what she says because for long periods she hardly speaks: 'She was always more inclined to silence when feeling most strongly.' Instead she observes, and the things that she observes are crucial things that largely pass the other characters by. It was with Fanny's 'rambling fancy' in mind that I wrote this book.

Chapter One
Steventon: 'The cradle of her genius'

*She... loved nothing so well in the world as rolling down
the green slope at the back of the house.*
NORTHANGER ABBEY (Chapter 1)

This is where it all began, here in this field. I pick my way along
the grass verge, craning over the hedge, trying to get a good view
of Jane Austen's birthplace. A tanker lorry comes belting along
the lane, leaving me pushed up uncomfortably against the
thorns.

People from all over the world make their way to the
Hampshire village of Steventon to pay homage to one of
England's greatest writers, yet there are no facilities, no sign-
posts, no walkways or retail outlets, not even a pub. There never
were. If you wish to follow in Jane Austen's footsteps, you must
use your imagination and you must use it above all now, at the
beginning of the journey. Close your eyes and imagine that here
in this field before you is a rectory. From this corner where you
stand, a carriage drive leads up to a front door with a latticed
porch. The house has two storeys and dormer attic windows,
and at the back there are two projecting wings, looking out onto
a garden that slopes up to a terrace walk. There are a lot of trees,

including some handsome elms and sycamores, and a shrubbery, flower beds, a vegetable garden. Behind the house a path leads uphill towards the church, hidden in the trees beyond.

It was in this house that Jane Austen was born, on 16 December 1775. The story of her early life has been told many times. She was the seventh of eight children and had one sister, Cassandra, to whom she was close all her life. Her father was rector of Steventon and also had the living of the nearby village of Deane. It was at Deane that the Reverend and Mrs Austen (George and Cassandra) began married life after their wedding in Bath in 1764. Their first three sons, James, George and Edward, were born at Deane, and when the living at Steventon became vacant the family packed up and made the short journey to their new home in 1771. According to Jane's nephew James Edward Austen-Leigh, in his *A Memoir of Jane Austen* (1870), 'Mrs Austen, who was not then in strong health, performed the short journey on a feather-bed, placed upon some soft articles of furniture in the waggon which held their household goods', for the road was a 'mere cart track, so cut up by deep ruts as to be impassable for a light carriage'.[1]

Steventon still lies deep in the Hampshire countryside, though it is certainly not cut off from road traffic. It sits in a triangular oasis bounded by the throbbing arteries of the M3 motorway, the A303 dual carriageway and the railway line from London to Southampton. Barely four miles away are the thrusting office blocks of Basingstoke. There's an air of prosperity in the small towns and lanes of this part of Hampshire.

I made my way to Steventon via Alresford early one Sunday morning, when the locals were already up and strolling home from the Tesco Metro, copies of the *Sunday Telegraph* furled round bottles of milk or wine in their carrier bags. In the fields walkers strode along footpaths, smoking cigars. Passing beneath the traffic hurtling along the M3, I approached Steventon down a lane from the village of North Waltham, slowing down for a man walking in the road, camouflage trousers tucked into his boots, a spaniel at each heel. Yellow fields of oilseed rape spread luminously against the grey skies. At the crossroads outside the village a four-fingered signpost leaned drunkenly, as if someone had been trying to twizzle it round to confuse an enemy.

Steventon is a tiny village of neat cottages strung out along both sides of the lane. A sign at the village entrance warns of deer. There's a bus shelter and a little Montessori nursery school stands nearby, but the place seems all but deserted. It would have been blissfully quiet but for the continual throb of light air-craft overhead, piloted by weekend fliers from a nearby airfield. This place was the centre of Jane Austen's world for the first 25 years of her life.

After being breast-fed by her mother for three months or so after her birth, baby Jane was sent to live with a woman else-where in the village, probably shortly after her christening in April 1776. She remained there for a year or 18 months, return-ing to her family permanently only when she could easily be managed at home. This practice, a not uncommon one for many genteel families of the time, seems harsh to modern sen-sibilities, with all our notions about the bonding process between mother and child. It disturbed even some contempo-rary commentators. In her account of Jane's childhood Claire Tomalin quotes William Cobbett on the subject: 'Who has not seen these banished children when brought and put into the arms of their mother, screaming to get from them and stretching out their little hands to get back to the arms of the nurse?'[2]

For Mrs Austen, however, it was a highly practical solution, which she probably adopted with few pangs. A busy clergyman's wife, with six other children to bring up, a house and a school to run, servants to supervise, and livestock to husband, she certainly did not have the time to provide the intense supervision that toddlers require. Her children grew up healthy at a time when the mortality rate for infants under five was still very high. But what about their emotional health? What about Jane? Claire Tomalin believes that this early separation had a lasting effect on her, and that this is manifested by a defensiveness and a lack of tenderness in her letters: 'They are the letters of someone who does not open her heart; and in the adult who avoids intimacy you sense the child who was uncertain where to expect love or to look for security, and armoured herself against rejection.'[3]

One of Jane's brothers suffered a greater misfortune. The Austens' second son, George, was born epileptic, and possibly deaf and dumb. At an early age he was sent away to be cared for, and Jane never mentions him (at least in the letters that survive). His family throughout his life paid for his upkeep and he lived to 72, a much riper age than his younger sister. For much of his life he lodged with his uncle, Mrs Austen's younger brother Thomas Leigh, who was also handicapped in some way.

In a much more fortunate turn of fate, Jane's elder brother Edward, born the year after George in 1767, was adopted at the age of 16 by a distant but wealthy cousin, Thomas Knight, and his wife, and thus became heir to Godmersham Park in Kent, as well as to substantial estates in and around Steventon, and elsewhere in Hampshire. Throughout their lives both Jane and Cassandra made frequent trips to Kent to stay with her brother, his wife and their 11 children. The eldest, Fanny Austen Knight, was to become Jane's favourite among her many nieces.

Steventon itself was no rural idyll in the late 18th century. Many of its inhabitants lived in extreme poverty, exacerbated by disease, bad weather and poor harvests. Charitable works were expected of a clergyman's daughter, so, accordingly, we find Jane itemizing her 'charities to the poor' to Cassandra in December 1798: 'I have given a pair of Worsted stockings to Mary Hutchins, Dame Kew, Mary Steevens & Dame Staples, and a shift to Hannah Staples, and a shawl to Betty Dawkins; amount ing in all to about half a guinea.' Rural crime was also rife, as Jane's biographer David Nokes discovered when he delved into the Hampshire archives for 1782, uncovering a catalogue of seri- ous felonies, including highway robbery, rape, burglary, house breaking, sodomy and bestiality; the murder of illegitimate chil- dren seems to have been alarmingly common too.[4]

For all this Jane seems to have had a largely unclouded child- hood. Her formal education took place largely at home in Steventon. She and Cassandra were sent away to school twice. The first time was when Jane was aged only seven, to an estab- lishment in Oxford. Before long the school moved to Southampton, where troops returning from abroad brought an infectious fever with them. Both sisters became ill – Jane dan- gerously so – and were brought home to recover. They didn't go back. Later the sisters spent some time at a school in Reading, but perhaps it proved too expensive, because they were home again for good in a matter of months.

In any case there must have been plenty of opportunities for learning at home. Jane's parents ran a small boys' school at the rectory to supplement their income. The number of boys, Claire

Tomalin says, was 'small enough for the Austens to run the school as a large family rather than as an institution'.[5] Some of the pupils became lifelong friends of the family. Jane grew up, then, with not only four older brothers around her, but lots of other boys as well. The rough and tumble must have been quite something. It's pleasing to think that Jane's early years might have inspired the passage at the beginning of *Northanger Abbey* in which she describes Catherine Morland's childhood as one of ten, three of them older brothers:

> She was fond of all boys' plays, and greatly preferred cricket, not merely to dolls, but to the more heroic enjoyments of infancy... she was moreover noisy and wild, hated confinement and cleanliness, and loved nothing so well in the world as rolling down the green slope at the back of the house.

The slope at the back of Jane's own childhood home in Steventon is still there, green and tempting.

When they got older and grew out of rolling, the Austen children entertained themselves by putting on theatrical productions in the barn in the field across the road from the rectory. Later, when Jane's elder brothers began to leave home to go their separate ways – James to Oxford, Edward to be groomed for the life of a landed gentleman and Francis away to sea – the rectory filled up again with other visitors, among them Jane's exotic cousin Eliza de Feuillide, who was later to marry her brother Henry. Eliza had spent much of her young life abroad and had married a French aristocrat, with whom she had a young son. Her stories of the wider world must have entranced the young Jane. In 1794 Eliza's husband was arrested and guillotined.

Jane Austen has been taken to task by some critics for not mentioning any of the turbulent events of the wider world in her novels. Whatever her reasons for not doing so, in her own life such events must have seemed all too real. Apart from the cruel fate that befell her cousin's husband, she had two brothers enduring danger and hardship on active service in the Royal Navy during the Napoleonic Wars. News from Frank and Charles was often agonizingly slow to arrive. On 24 January 1809 Jane wrote of having just received a letter from Charles, sent from Bermuda early the previous December.

Despite such worries, there was always plenty to occupy Jane at home. There's quite a lot going on in Steventon today too, if the parish magazine I picked up in the church is anything to go by. A busy social network thrives both here and in the surrounding villages. The magazine advertised a whole series of forthcoming events: the village fete, a gymkhana, an oyster festival, a recital of 'American Songs and Operatic Arias', and a 'Ladies' Breakfast' in Steventon Village Hall. There were details of recent births and marriages, mobile library visits, and bulk oil deliveries. Children were being invited to play rounders on the Cuckoo Meadow in North Waltham. There was plenty of activity in Jane Austen's time too, although her world was a less socially blended one, of course. Jane's circle of friends and acquaintances resided in the manor houses and rectories of Steventon and the neighbouring towns and villages. You can still peer at some of them behind their high walls and hedges if you follow the footpaths around the parish today: nearby Deane House, for instance, with its gravel drive and its sign saying 'Extra Slow: Children and Dogs'; or Ashe Park, a large red-brick Jacobean mansion now in private hands, where charity polo matches take place and Ashe Park bottled mineral water is produced. According to the website of Well, Well, Well, the owner and bottler of the brand, the water at Ashe Park was 'revered for centuries before Jane Austen became a regular visitor to the house'. 'In fact', it continues, 'she wrote *Pride and Prejudice* in what is now the drawing room of the house.'[6] This strikes me as highly unlikely: Jane's love of privacy when writing is well-known.

However, Jane did frequently attend balls and supper parties in the great houses and assembly rooms of the district. James Edward Austen-Leigh writes in his *Memoir* of 1870:

> There must have been more dancing throughout the country in those days than there is now Many country towns had a monthly ball throughout the winter, in some of which the same apartment served for dancing and tea-room. Dinner parties more frequently ended with an extempore dance on the carpet, to the music of a harpsichord in the house, or a fiddle from the village.[7]

Jane described such gatherings to Cassandra when the sisters were apart, keen to keep her sister up with all the gossip. Here she is in December 1798 reporting on a ball held locally: 'There were twenty Dances & I danced them all & without any fatigue… in cold weather & with few couples I fancy I could just as well dance for a week together as for half an hour.' A few weeks later, in January 1799, she attended a ball at nearby Kempshott Park:

> I wore my Green shoes last night and took my white fan with me… There was one Gentleman, an officer of the

Cheshire, a very good looking Man who I was told very much wanted to be introduced to me; – but as he did not want it quite enough to take much trouble in effecting it, We never did bring it about.

She is at her astringent best in a letter of November 1800, describing a ball at grand Hurstbourne Park, near Whitchurch, the home of the Earl of Portsmouth, a former pupil of her father's, who was later declared insane. 'I believe I drank too much wine last night', she begins, and then proceeds to describe some of her fellow guests: 'Mrs Blount... appeared exactly as she did in September with the same broad face, diamond bandeau, white shoes, pink husband, & fat neck'; 'The Miss Maitlands are both prettyish... with brown skins, large dark eyes, & a good deal of nose'; 'Miss Debary, Susan and Sally made their appearance... and I was as civil to them as their bad breath would allow.'

Everyone who pictures Jane Austen as a demure creature, sitting quietly in a corner with her sewing – men seem to be particularly prone to this view – should read her letters, in which such observations are not uncommon. In October 1798, to give another example, Jane wrote to Cassandra from Steventon: 'Mrs Hall of Sherbourn was brought to bed yesterday of a dead child, some weeks before she expected, oweing to a fright. I suppose she happened unawares to look at her husband.'

Did Jane ever repent of her acid tongue?

Up a lane, some distance from the rest of the village, is Steventon's parish church, dedicated to St Nicholas, where Jane's

father officiated for 30 years and the rest of the family wor-
shipped. Remarkably for such an isolated building, it is left open
every day and, though I didn't see another soul, the ancient
church is visited by Jane Austen readers from across the world.
Much of the money for its restoration has come from devoted
donors in far-flung places.

Jane Austen would recognize its squat tower immediately,
although the spire would surprise her as it dates only from
Victorian times. It is topped with a weather vane in the shape of
a quill, in tribute to Jane. As you step into the church's chilly
interior from the small entrance porch, an arcade of three
arches faces you above the nave, adorned with painted Victorian
decorations. According to the local historian Henry Henshaw,
writing in 1949, the keystones of the chancel arch separated
slightly when the church shook with the impact of the German
bombs dropping on nearby North Waltham in 1940.[8] In the
chancel itself there are memorials to the Reverend James Austen,
Jane's eldest brother, who succeeded his father as rector of
Steventon, and his two wives, Anne and Mary. The most moving tablet of all, however, is a heart-breaking wall monument in
memory of the three daughters of the Reverend William Knight,
Jane's nephew and another rector of Steventon. Mary Agnes,
aged five, Cecilia, aged four, and Augusta, aged three, all died of
scarlet fever in June 1848, the younger two on the same day.
'Lovely and pleasant in their lives, and in their death they were
not divided' reads the verse, inspired by II Samuel, Chapter 1,
verse 23, in which David laments the deaths of Saul and
Jonathan.

Today these Bible verses may well strike all but the most
devout as scant consolation for such a calamity. In earlier times,

they would have seemed far more categorical. Though they concentrate almost entirely on the here and now, just occasionally Jane Austen's letters remind us how unshakeable was her belief – and that of most of her contemporaries – in an afterlife, to be spent with God in Heaven. After her sister-in-law Elizabeth died in October 1808 she wrote to Cassandra that their brother Edward had 'a religious mind to bear him up, & a Disposition that will gradually lead him to comfort'. Cassandra herself wrote shortly after Jane's death: 'God grant that I may never cease to reflect on her as inhabiting Heaven & never cease my humble endeavours (when it shall please God) to join her there.'[9]

There is a tiny pipe organ in the church and, by the door, a wooden vestry, which, in its original position at the front of the church, served as the box pew for the local gentry, the Digweeds of Steventon Manor. A family well known to the Austens, its various members are commemorated by inscriptions along the nave's tiled floor. When I visited the church, brass vases filled with daffodils and arum lilies stood on the altar, and grass sprouted from an Easter garden up a model Calvary. By the lectern hangs a blue banner with a black felt silhouette of Jane Austen, and someone has worked matching kneelers. The Bible on the lectern was open at John, Chapters 16 and 17: 'Look, the hour is coming, has indeed already come, when you are all to be scattered, each to his home, leaving me alone.'

Jane must have spent a lot of time here. When she was young her indulgent father even allowed her to scribble in the parish register. On forms for the publication of banns of marriage Jane made up three entries in which she tried the names of imaginary prospective husbands on for size: 'The banns of marriage between Henry Frederic Howard Fitzwilliam of London and

Jane Austen of Steventon'; 'Edmund Arthur William Mortimer of Liverpool and Jane Austen of Steventon were married in this church'; 'This marriage was solemnized by us, by Jack Smith & Jane Smith, late Austen' ('A Mrs Smith!', as Sir Walter Elliot in *Persuasion* would have sneered).

Jane never did marry, of course. Her near misses have been the subject of endless speculation, not least her early flirtation or serious romance – depending on your point of view – with a man named Tom Lefroy, whom she met at nearby Ashe. The rectory there was the home of Tom's aunt, Madame Lefroy, who was a friend and mentor of the young Jane. Jane's earliest surviving letters date from the period when Tom Lefroy was staying at Ashe in 1796. In a letter to her sister in January 1796 Jane jokes: 'He is a very gentlemanlike, good-looking, pleasant young man... he has but one fault... it is that his morning coat is a great deal too light.' A few days later she writes: 'I mean to confine myself in future to Mr Tom Lefroy, for whom I donot [*sic*] care sixpence.' Within days, however, Tom departs: 'At length the Day is come when I am to flirt my last with Tom Lefroy, & when you receive this it will be over – My tears flow as I write, at the melancholy idea.' There was clearly a spark between the two of them, but Jane's letter is so cheerful and light-hearted that it is difficult to feel that she took the idea of a romance with Tom Lefroy seriously. Some biographers think that the unsuitability of the match, Jane having so little money, led Tom's relatives to separate the two of them. This may have been the case, but, personally, I find it hard to credit that the sudden termination of their friendship had any lasting effects on Jane. By this time she was already in thrall to her one true love: writing.

Jane's teenage compositions were comic ones, and they are still enormous fun to read today. Some were originally written down in a notebook inscribed '*Ex dono mei Patris*', a gift from the father who always encouraged her in her writing. For her 19th birthday he was to make her a present of a small mahogany writing desk, which she christened by writing her novel *Lady Susan*. This same writing desk almost ended up on the other side of the world. In 1798, having been left at the Bull and George at Dartford, en route from Kent to Steventon, the desk was accidentally put into another chaise and 'driven off towards Gravesend on their way to the West Indies', but happily the desk, together with Jane's dressing boxes, was quickly retrieved by a man on a horse. [10]

Love and Freindship [*sic*], written in 1790, is a short epistolary novel in which Jane took great pleasure in satirizing the overblown romantic fiction of the day. It is full of ridiculous coincidences, women who faint repeatedly on sofas and girls who disobey their parents. One character even says: 'Where in the name of wonder did you pick up this unmeaning gibberish? You have been studying novels I suspect.' In *Lesley Castle*, composed in the early part of 1792 when Jane was 16, there are more comic capers. The fiancé of Charlotte Lutterell's sister Eloisa is thrown from his horse and their impending wedding has to be called off, much to Charlotte's chagrin. She has spent days preparing the wedding breakfast, only to have the 'mortification of finding that I had been Roasting, Broiling and Stewing both the Meat and Myself to no purpose'. Despite the death of the prospective bridegroom, the family gets stuck into the food in an attempt to clear the pantry.

By the time Tom Lefroy left Hampshire for good, in early 1796 – Jane never saw him again – *Elinor and Marianne*, the first version of the novel that became *Sense and Sensibility*, had already been written, and the composition of *First Impressions*, later *Pride and Prejudice*, was under way. Jane was to write a third novel at Steventon: *Susan*, composed in 1798–9 and published much later under the title *Northanger Abbey*. Claire Tomalin believes that the Lefroy 'affair' was a painful blow for the young Jane: '… just at that moment you feel she might quite cheerfully have exchanged her genius for the prospect of being married to Tom Lefroy one day… with a large family of children to bring up'.[11] Jane's novels became her children. In 1811, with the publication of *Sense and Sensibility* finally in sight, she was to write: 'No indeed, I am never too busy to think of S&S. I can no more forget it, than a mother can forget her sucking child.'

At the time I was in Steventon a film company had embarked on shooting a £9 million production entitled *Becoming Jane*, based on the notion that Jane was a romantic who had been inspired to write her greatest works by her thwarted love affair with Tom. Quoted in *The Times* in March 2006, Tom's first cousin four times removed, Mrs Helen Lefroy, said of the film: 'What people don't wish to note is that after he met Jane, he became engaged to the sister of his college friend… a simple, biddable girl. People of his ability didn't want intellectuals. He wanted a housekeeper.'[12]

Jane was still only 20 in 1796, and there was every prospect that she would find someone to marry. At least one firm offer did later come her way, but in the early 19th century the chances of finding a husband whom she could love, but who would also allow her the freedom to write and give full flow to her genius, were slim indeed. It is futile to speculate how Jane really felt later in life about being single and childless. We, however, are fortunate indeed that she was left free to devote her time to the off-spring of her pen.

In St Nicholas's Church generations of real children have been baptized in the 19th-century white marble font, which boasts a new oak cover, carved by a local craftsman and dedicated on 9 July 2000. A notice acknowledges the gratitude of the rector and parishioners to the members of the Wisconsin region of the Jane Austen Society of North America (JASNA) for their generous contribution to the making of the cover, which depicts a Saxon cross and a monk at prayer, a sheep at his side. The beautifully carved shaft of the real Saxon cross that inspired this design sits by the pulpit. It was found in the wall of the nearby Tudor manor house before it was demolished in 1970.

Close by and so low down that it is easy to miss is a display of the original parts of the pump that stood over the well in the backyard of the rectory. These few bits of metal are all that remains today of the place where Jane wrote her novels.

That's the strange thing about being in Steventon Church. At first glance there are few outward signs that you are in a place of huge significance. It's an ancient and pretty country church, but little distinguishes it from similar ecclesiastical buildings all over the South of England. But sit in the back pew, as I did, and open the visitors' book, and the comments of hundreds of visitors pour from its pages. For literary pilgrims their comments are pretty prosaic: 'Lovely', 'Nice', 'Peaceful', 'PeacFul' [*sic*], 'Nice', 'Beutiful' [*sic*], 'Brilliant', 'Important', 'Fab' and 'Well worth the walk' were typical recent examples. Perhaps many visitors are both weary and awed, having come so far: from Russia, South Africa, Nigeria, Iceland, Australia, Japan, Sweden and Brazil, as well as from almost every state in the United States and every part of Britain. I turned the pages back a bit further. Someone from Weymouth had visited with his 'emotional girlfriend'. Someone thought that the church was 'spooky'; someone else thought it was 'cool'. Some comments were religious: 'A very special day. Thanks Lord.' Others were downright surreal: 'All advice is useless.' 'I just wanted to see something she saw' said someone else. Charlie from Basingstoke had written: 'Where's the toilet? Where's the pub?'

From the small bookstall I bought a guidebook and some postcards. There were no Jane Austen pens left, but you could buy a CD of *Music from Jane Austen's Church*, a recording of a concert here in 2003, with a programme of 30 pieces of music for harpsichord, organ, trumpet and voices performed by the rector, the organist and members of the choir. Closing the programme is a prayer written by Jane Austen that has been set to music: 'Give us Grace Almighty Father, so to pray, as to deserve to be heard, to address thee with our hearts as well as our lips.'

Jane wrote only a handful of prayers. For years I've had a card with a passage from one of them stuck to the mirror on my dressing table. I bought it at a church in Somerset, completely unconnected with Jane Austen: 'Incline us Oh God! To Think humbly of ourselves, to be severe only in the examination of our own conduct, to consider our fellow-creatures with kindness, and to judge of all they say and do with that charity which we would desire from them ourselves.' Not a bad maxim for life, whether one is religious or not. In the light of some of her more acid comments about people, I find it particularly comforting that Jane Austen found her own exhortation to 'consider our fellow creatures with kindness' and 'judge them with charity' as difficult to stick to as the rest of us do.

It would be a mistake to assume that Jane's upbringing as the daughter of a clergyman was an overly pious one, for her father seems to have been rather liberal by the standards of the day. For one thing, he allowed her, from an early age (she could read well, it seems, from the age of eight) to read any book that took her fancy among his extensive library of 500 volumes. Accordingly Jane's reading was eclectic, encompassing history, poetry, books in French and all the popular novels of the day, many of which had extremely racy subject matter: drunkenness, rapes, murders, elopements, adulterous liaisons and bigamous marriages are legion. Writing in 1817, the year of Jane's death, her brother Henry Austen recalled: 'It is difficult to say at what age she was not intimately acquainted with the merits and defects of the best essays and novels in the English language.'[13] Jane read works by Fielding, Defoe, Swift, Johnson, Goldsmith, Fanny Burney, Sterne, Ann Radcliffe and Samuel Richardson, who was one of her preferred writers. His sprawling novel *Sir Charles Grandison* is said to have been her favourite. The ghastly Isabella Thorpe in *Northanger Abbey* calls it 'an amazing horrid book', so Jane must have liked it.

Novels were the preferred reading matter of the whole Austen family. In December 1798, after Jane received a note from a Mrs Martin asking her to become a subscriber to her new lending library, she commented in a letter to Cassandra: 'Mrs Martin tells us that her Collection is not to consist only of Novels, but of every kind of Literature... She might have spared this pretension to our family who are great Novel-readers & not ashamed of being so.'

Throughout Jane's work characters damn themselves merely by proclaiming that they never read novels. There is John

Thorpe in *Northanger Abbey*: 'Oh Lord! Not I; I never read novels; I have something else to do... they are the stupidest things in creation.' (Henry Tilney by contrast declares: 'The person, gentleman or lady who has not pleasure in a good novel must be intolerably stupid.') In *Pride and Prejudice* it is Mr Collins who protests that he never reads them, remarking: 'I have often observed how little young ladies are interested by books of a serious stamp.' In *Persuasion* Anne's sister, the snobbish Elizabeth, returns a book to Lady Russell unread: 'You may as well take back that tiresome book she would lend me, and pretend I have read it through. I really cannot be plaguing myself for ever with all the new poems and states of the nation that come out. Lady Russell quite bores one with her new publications.' In *Mansfield Park*, while Fanny Price has been a collector of books 'from the first hour of her commanding a shilling', her suitor, Henry Crawford, has the ability to perform speeches from Shakespeare well, but hasn't actually read any of the plays. He is all show, as events will later prove. Unlike Fanny's sister Susan, no one could ever say of the Austen family that 'the early habit of reading was wanting'.

However, Jane was not always stuck indoors writing or with her head in a book. In the days when genteel single women were not supposed to go anywhere unchaperoned, the freedom to roam must have been particularly precious to her. Though her novels rarely describe nature and landscape, Jane seems to have been fond of walking in the countryside around Steventon, even in bad weather. In December 1798 she wrote: 'I enjoyed the hard black Frosts of last week very much, and one day while they lasted walked to Deane by myself.' Such was the roughness of the roads that even a prolonged spell of rain could isolate a village such as Steventon from the outside world for days. In October 1798 Jane wrote: 'There has been a great deal of rain here for this last fortnight... Steventon lane has its full share of it, & I donot know when I shall be able to get to Deane.'

Jane Austen's heroines are not easily deterred from country walking. In *Pride and Prejudice* Elizabeth Bennett walks the three miles to the Bingleys' house to visit her sister Jane, who is laid up with a severe chill. She crosses 'field after field at a quick pace, jumping over stiles and springing over puddles with impatient activity', arriving at Netherfield 'with weary ancles, dirty stockings, and a face glowing with all the warmth of exercise'. Caroline Bingley and her sister Mrs Hurst are all disdain. 'Why must she be scampering about the country because her sister has a cold?'. 'Yes, and her petticoat; I hope you saw her petticoat, six inches deep in mud.' Miss Bingley tries to goad Mr Darcy into expressing his disapproval: 'To walk three miles, or four miles, or five miles, or whatever it is, above her ancles in dirt, and alone, quite alone! What could she mean by it? It seems to me to shew an abominable sort of conceited independence, a most country town indifference to decorum.' Darcy retorts that it shows 'an affection for her sister that is very pleasing', adding for good measure his observation that her 'fine eyes' had been brightened by the exercise.

As I came out of the church I looked up at the medieval bells, restored to working order in 1995 after many years of silence with donations from American and Canadian members of the JASNA. It was very tempting to pull one of the striped ropes and hear the sound that had called Jane to church of a Sunday morning. Outside, the churchyard was carpeted with primroses and thistles. I picked my way through the long damp grass, and found the lichen-covered tomb of Jane's brother James and his wife Mary, its inscription almost illegible. Round the front again, I stopped to admire the 900-year-old yew tree that stands guard by the church door. Once upon a time the huge wrought-iron key to the church was kept in its hollow trunk, but it disappeared mysteriously some years ago and its replacement is kept elsewhere.

I walked away down Church Walk, as generations of parishioners have done after morning service. It was deserted. Once there were full congregations every Sunday. Now only a couple of services are held here each month and the rector officiates at three other churches as well. Rabbits dived for cover in a nearby field at the sound of my approach, while on the other side of the lane a pair of beautiful thoroughbreds with coats on whinnied emphatically and tossed their manes. At the T-junction where you turn left for Steventon village, I stared again at the site of the old rectory among the chestnut trees in the field on my right. Across the road, on top of a nearby rise, is the imposing front of Steventon House, the building that replaced it as rectory, built by Jane's brother Edward in 1826. Its elevated position was, I suppose, more in keeping with the social position of the new rector, Edward's son William, though not even these genteel new surroundings could prevent the tragic deaths of his three little daughters.

When Constance Hill, the author of *Jane Austen: Her Homes and Her Friends* came here in the early 1900s, she managed to find an old man leaning on a garden gate in the village who claimed to remember the old rectory: 'I was a little 'un when the old house was pulled down, but I well recollect seeing the bricks and rubbish lyin' about on the ground.' Her informant was a man by the name of Littleworth, whose grandfather had been coachman to Jane's brother James and whose mother was a god-daughter of Jane's. His grandmother, known as Nanny Littleworth, may even have been the foster mother who looked after the Austen children as babies. At the time of Constance Hill's visit the aforementioned pump still stood in the field, a remnant of the old washhouse behind the rectory. Even that has now gone.[14]

In the corner of the field, however, stands a lime tree. In January 1813, long after Jane and her parents had moved away, James Austen, who succeeded his father as rector of Steventon, planted the lime tree with his son, James Edward, who was then 14. Something of an aspiring writer himself, James penned the following lines on the occasion:

> This tree which we together plant,
> If Heaven a parent's wishes grant,
> For many a future year shall prove
> A record of our mutual love.
> While you, my boy, at school or college
> Are absent, gaining useful knowledge
> Oft to this tree shall I repair
> And in my fancy meet you there...[15]

James Edward Austen-Leigh, the young son for whom the lime tree was planted, was to become Jane's first biographer, publishing *A Memoir of Jane Austen* in 1870. Jane recorded his birth in a letter of November 1798: 'Mary was brought to bed last night, at eleven o'clock of a fine little boy, and everything is going on very well.' Jane was never fond of his mother, her sister-in-law Mary. A week or so later, after visiting her and the new baby, Jane remarks cattily: 'Mary does not manage matters in such a way as to make me want to lay in myself. She is not tidy enough in her appearance; she has no dressing-gown to sit up in; her curtains are all too thin.'

Besides the lime there are few other trees in the field today, but in a drawing of the rectory made from memory by Jane's niece Anna the house is surrounded by them. In his *Memoir* Anna's brother James Edward remembers that it 'stood in a shallow valley, surrounded by sloping meadows, well sprinkled with elm trees'.[16] Thousands of elms disappeared forever from the English landscape during the 1960s and 1970s, the victims of Dutch elm disease. The elms at Steventon, however, met their fate much earlier. On Sunday 9 November 1800 Jane reported to Cassandra that there had been a 'dreadful storm of wind... which has done a great deal of mischief among our trees. – I was sitting alone in the dining room, when an odd kind of crash startled me – in a moment afterwards it was repeated; I then went to the window, which I reached just in time to see the last of our two highly valued Elms descend into the Sweep!!!!!' (Nowhere else does Jane use even two exclamation marks.) Several other elms in the meadow were likewise blown down, along with a maypole and a weathercock in the garden. Jane particularly regretted the demise of 'three elms which grew in Hall's meadow & gave such ornament to it'.

Jane mentions a number of improvements that were made to the rectory garden in her letters, including some turfing, and the planting of lilacs, beech, ash and larch trees. There was a debate about whether to create an orchard or a plantation of larch, mountain ash and acacia on the right-hand side of the elm walk: but that was before the storm. Today all trace of the garden that inspired so much thought has gone, although, according to the village historian Henry Henshaw, snowdrops still persisted in the field in 1949, evidence of planting some 150 years before.[17]

As you drive northwards out of Steventon, you pass through a long tunnel under the railway. If Jane Austen had lived to a reasonably old age, she would have had the opportunity to try train travel. It must have been a revelation for someone used to bumping along in a carriage at six miles per hour. The first train to make the journey straight through from London to Southampton steamed past Steventon on 11 May 1840. According to Henry Henshaw, this maiden journey was celebrated by the roasting of a bullock at nearby Micheldever Station. Part of the roast was brought to Steventon and 'consumed by the villagers with great enjoyment'.[18] Soon regular trains were passing across the top of the embankment just outside the village, from which passengers could look down from under their umbrellas (the first carriages were open to the elements) on the thatched roofs and cart tracks of Steventon. The remote rural existence that its inhabitants had lived out for centuries was changing, their horizons being pushed slowly but inexorably out beyond the parish boundaries.

Jane's own horizons had long extended beyond the confines of Steventon. She had ambitions that circumstances forced her to nurture in obscurity for most of her life, but she was not alone in believing that she had a talent that deserved to be shared. In November 1797 her father wrote to the publisher Thomas

Cadell in London, offering him the manuscript of *First Impressions*. The refusal came quickly: 'Declined By Return of Post.'[19] More fool Cadell. After her father's death Jane's favourite brother Henry took up her cause. Finally, in 1813, *Pride and Prejudice*, as it had become, was published, never to go out of print.

In 1800 Jane's parents decided to retire and move to Bath. The contrast between agrarian life in a remote Hampshire village and the social whirl of Bath could not be greater. It's understandable that so many versions of her life conclude that the change was a distressing one for her, yet, after re-reading Jane's surviving letters from her last few years in Steventon, it seems easier to believe that, contrary to the received wisdom, it was a very welcome change for her. Her circle at Steventon was composed of the same people, year in, year out, and the increasingly intolerant comments in her letters strongly suggest that she was becoming creatively frustrated with the incestuousness of country life. She longed to spread her wings, and find new inspirations and fresh material to work with. Perhaps she might even see her writing published at last. It seems to me that Nigel Nicolson got it right in a lecture he gave in 2002, entitled *Was Jane Austen Happy in Bath?*[20]

> Steventon, after all, had ceased to be the cheerful family home of her childhood and early youth. Her four brothers had left it to start their careers… and their parents were growing too old to undertake the manifold duties of a country parish. Local society was too small to offer Jane much variety, and the Basingstoke balls were beginning to lose their appeal. It is not difficult to imagine the dreariness of long winter nights in deep country,

with no entertainment in the ramshackle rectory except
what the four of them could provide for each other.

A few short weeks after her parents announced their plans Jane
wrote in January 1801: 'We have lived long enough in this
Neighbourhood… It must not be generally known that I am not
sacrificing a great deal in quitting the Country – or I can expect
to inspire no tenderness, no interest in those we leave behind.'
It seems clear that, aside from some natural regrets at leaving her
childhood home, Jane was actually rather relieved to be going.
David Nokes sums up her feelings in his imaginative biography
of Jane. 'Such a woman was cursed with dreams and aspirations
which soared far beyond the homely routines of a handful of
Hampshire rural villages; yet with a sensibility too rational for
romantic fantasies of escape.' [21]

I left Steventon in search of lunch and stopped just up the
road at the Deane Gate pub, a former coaching inn that sits
right on the busy B3400, the road from Basingstoke to Andover,
its whitewashed walls spattered with the dirt of exhaust fumes.
The Deane Gate was once Steventon's gateway to the wider
world. Not only was it a stopping place for coaches going to
London, Bath and Exeter, but it was also the dropping-off point
for letters for the residents of Steventon. In January 1799 Jane's
younger brother Charles, a lieutenant in the Royal Navy, who
had been recalled to his ship off the coast of Kent, encountered
some problems getting back to London: 'Charles attempted to
go to town last night, and got as far on his road thither as Deane
Gate; but both the coaches were full, and we had the pleasure of
seeing him back again.'

Both mail and stage coaches stopped at Deane Gate in those
days. Mail coaches, run by the government as part of the postal

service, were able to carry up to four passengers as well as mail-bags, as long as they didn't have any luggage. The were pulled by four horses, driven by a coachman who rode with an armed guard next to him in case of highwaymen, and travelled at seven to eight miles an hour. Stage coaches were run by private firms. They were pulled by six to eight horses and could seat six passengers inside and as many on the roof as could cling on to the handles provided, their legs dangling over the edge. It must have been an astonishingly uncomfortable way to travel, particularly in bad weather. Because of their top-heaviness, stage coaches were involved in frequent accidents. In her book *Jane Austen: The World of Her Novels,* Deirdre Le Faye mentions that when the Gosport coach overturned in 1795 it was carrying eleven passengers on the coach and box, not including the driver, and nine in the basket at the back designed for luggage.[22]

The horses suffered too. Though they were changed at frequent staging posts throughout each journey, in practice they were often cruelly whipped and literally worked to death in order to keep the coaches running on time. Deirdre Le Faye writes of one firm set up in London in 1816 to run a service from London to Brighton at a guaranteed travelling time of six hours for the 52-mile gallop. It went out of business, however, after 15 of its horses died in one week.[23] You still see horses everywhere in this part of Hampshire today, though mercifully they are no longer required to drag public transport. Many belt along inside horseboxes at several times the speed their ancestors once galloped down the same roads.

Highway robbery was another hazard faced by travellers during Jane Austen's time. Deirdre Le Faye writes that during the summer of 1793 a highwayman lurked in the woods only a few miles from Steventon, robbing passing carriages over a period of months before the offer of a large reward for his capture made him leave the district, though not before he had robbed a friend of the Austens, Mrs Bramston of Oakley Hall, who parted with eight guineas after the highwayman threatened to blow her brains out.[24]

Constance Hill stayed at Deane Gate in 1902, the night before she visited Steventon. She and her sister Ellen, who contributed the drawings to Constance's book, had been turned away from another inn just up the road, so it was with some relief that they found lodgings at the Deane Gate: 'Our troubles were now over, and much we enjoyed our cosy supper, which we ate in a tiny parlour of spotless cleanliness.'[25]

The dining area at the Deane Gate today is large and open-plan, and has the kind of traditional, slightly faded pub interior less often found in these days of 'gastro-pubs' and themed chains. There are horse brasses on the walls and the carpet design swirls around you as Neil Diamond croons from the speakers. A notice reads 'Save Water, Drink Beer' and in the Ladies a bottle of Elizabeth Arden's 'Provocative Women' body lotion has been left for the use of patrons. I juggled my plough-man's lunch with an Ordnance Survey map and my copy of Constance Hill's book. 'Could we have two roast lambs to start with?', said someone at the next table. Outside cars hurtled past on their way to Basingstoke, Andover and beyond. Ellen Hill's drawing of the Deane Gate in 1902 shows a family of chickens pecking unconcernedly around in the road. Today they would become roadkill in a matter of seconds, like all the other poor creatures that lie splattered on these Hampshire lanes.

Constance Hill wrote of her stay at the Deane Gate: 'A chat

with our landlady gave us the welcome intelligence that we were now within two miles of Steventon... So we fell asleep that night with the happy consciousness that we were really in Austen-land.'[26] What was it about this part of Hampshire that gave rise to such a woman and to such books? After all, Hampshire proudly proclaims itself 'Jane Austen Country' on the boundary signs as you cross into the county today. It is Austen-land still.

In his *Memoir,* James Edward Austen-Leigh wrote of Steventon: 'this was the residence of Jane Austen for twenty-five years. This was the cradle of her genius... In strolls along these wood-walks, thick-coming fancies rose in her mind, and gradually assumed the forms in which they came forth to the world.'[27] I gazed upon the same countryside, and realized that, however long I stared at the commonest of English natural productions, its grass, trees and hedgerows, I was never going to be assailed by the same 'thick-coming fancies'. Perhaps G.K. Chesterton had reached a similar conclusion when he wrote of Jane that she was not 'inflamed or inspired or even moved to be a genius; she simply was a genius. Her fire... began with herself; like the fire of the first man who rubbed two dry sticks together.'[28]

Steventon will always be famous as the place where Jane Austen was born and wrote the first versions of three of her novels. In some ways it's appropriate that there's so little to see for, when she left Steventon, she was eager for a wider world. Nevertheless, I hope that at least the snowdrops still flower on its green slopes, to prove that she was once there.

Chapter Two
Bath: 'Smoke and confusion'

For six weeks, I allow, Bath is pleasant enough; but beyond that it is the most tiresome place in the world.
NORTHANGER ABBEY (Chapter 10)

Jane Austen disliked Bath – or so almost everyone seems to believe. Even members of her own family later put it about that when Jane's parents announced, in late 1800, that they planned to leave the rectory at Steventon for good and move to Bath, Jane 'fainted away' with horror at the prospect.

I don't think Jane Austen disliked Bath at all, and I find the story of her fainting hard to believe too. After all, this was a woman who lampooned the whole swooning business in *Love and Freindship*, the epistolary novel she wrote when she was 14. The heroine, Laura, records the cautionary tale of her own life in letters to Marianne, the daughter of a friend: 'Beware of fainting-fits... Though at the time they may be refreshing and agreable yet beleive [*sic*] me they will in the end, if too often repeated and at improper seasons, prove destructive to your Constitution... Run mad as often as you chuse; but do not faint.'

To be sure, the prospect of leaving the only home you have ever known probably induces, at the very least, a feeling of apprehension, even at the age of 25. Yet the move to Bath was hardly a voyage into the unknown. Jane had visited the city several times before and for her parents, now aged 61 and 69, retirement in Bath may have been a long-standing intention. The city held happy memories: for one thing, it had been the venue for their marriage in 1764. Even if it came as a shock to her initially, within weeks Jane was making light of the move: 'We plan having a steady Cook, & a young giddy Housemaid, with a sedate, middle aged Man who is to undertake the double office of Husband to the former & sweetheart to the latter', she wrote in January 1801. So I went to Bath, already confident in my half-baked theory that Jane Austen's association with the city was not nearly as unhappy as it is generally claimed to have been.

Jane's relationship with Bath falls into two distinct phases: first, her acquaintance with the city as a visitor during the late 1790s; and then the period when Bath was her home, between 1801 and 1806. By the time the Austens took up residence in Bath, Jane had already completed her novel *Susan*, later revised and published as *Northanger Abbey*, the first half of which is set in the city. A large portion of the action in *Persuasion*, including the moving denouement, also takes place in Bath. The city also receives at least a mention in the other four of Jane Austen's major novels. In *Pride and Prejudice* Wickham takes himself off to Bath to enjoy himself and get away from his all too hasty marriage to Lydia Bennet. In *Emma* it is in Bath that Mr Elton, after his proposal to Emma has been rebuffed, finds a wife in the enticing shape of Miss Augusta Hawkins, with ten thousand a year. Whatever she actually thought of the place, the influence of the city on Jane Austen's writing cannot be denied.

Jane's first visit to Bath probably took place in November 1797. None of her correspondence survives from this period, but the visit is referred to specifically in later letters. It's likely that Jane stayed with her mother's wealthy, gout-ridden brother, James Leigh-Perrot, and his wife Jane, who spent at least half the year in Bath at their genteel address of no. 1 The Paragon. Whatever Jane got up to during this first visit, it certainly gave her some good material to work with, for she began writing *Susan* not long afterwards.

I arrived in Bath on a freezing weekend in early February when only a few tourists were mooching around. In Jane Austen's day February was the height of the 'season' and Bath would have been full to the gunnels. To help me get my bearings I followed the tourists and took a Bath Sightseeing Tour by open-top bus. 'Where are you from?' the driver asked. When he heard that I lived only 30 miles up the road he didn't bat an eyelid. Up on the top deck the cold was bitter even with the bus at a standstill: I huddled into my seat behind a Japanese man in an Edinburgh bobble hat and stuffed the headphones provided for the commentary under my own woolly number. The bus set off up the High Street. We passed Bath Abbey ('known as the lantern of England owing to its 52 windows – one for every week of the year') and the Guildhall (with its 'beautiful Banqueting Hall, built by Thomas Baldwin during the 1770s'). The Guildhall also houses the Bath and North East Somerset register office, and as we rumbled past a wedding party emerged. The raven-haired bride wore a fur-trimmed ivory gown and carried a bouquet of orange flowers. She looked ecstatic and, despite the cold, lingered outside with her groom, basking in the warmth of her big day.

The muffled commentary continued with a description of the development of Bath in the 18th century. From a small provincial town of 3,000 people, still confined within higgledy-piggledy medieval lines, it was transformed within a few short decades into England's most fashionable watering hole and a town second only to London in cultural importance. By the end of the century its population had swelled to 30,000 souls.

Bath's great attraction was, of course, its waters. The three thermal springs that rise through faults in the Mendip rocks to surface in the place where Bath now stands were already known to the Romans, who built a luxurious health resort called Aquae Sulis. In medieval times the springs were still in use and the most favoured of the three, closest to Bath Abbey, became known as the 'King's Spring', after King Henry I. The waters were still famed for their supposed curative powers six centuries later and the 18th-century developers of Bath sought to capitalize on their potential to pull in wealthy visitors. 'Many people have come to Bath, tired of taking medicines to no purpose at all', trumpeted the *Bath Guide* of 1800. 'They have drunk the Bath water with abundance of delight and pleasure, and by the help of a little physic have recovered to admiration.'[1]

A sojourn in Georgian Bath wasn't just about taking the waters, of course. As Mrs Allen remarks to Henry Tilney in *Northanger Abbey*: 'Well, sir, and I dare say you are not sorry to be back again for it is just the place for young people – and for everybody else too.' Mr Allen has been 'ordered to Bath for the benefit of a gouty constitution'. He will take the waters, leaving Mrs Allen and Catherine Morland free to enjoy 'all the difficulties and dangers of a six week residence in Bath'. For those accompanying relatives not incapacitated by ill health, a stay in Bath encompassed shopping, dancing, promenading, theatre-going and, above all, watching people and gossiping about them.

In the spring of 1799 Jane Austen was just such an accompanying relative. Edward Austen, Jane's brother and the wealthy adopted heir of the Knight family of Godmersham Park in Kent, was still suffering the bout of ill health that had troubled him throughout the previous winter. Jane had been less than sympathetic, remarking a trifle drily in a letter to Cassandra at Godmersham the previous December: 'Poor Edward! It is very hard that he who has everything else in the World that he can wish for, should not have good health too.' Edward was advised by his doctors to see what the curative waters of Bath might do for him, so, together with his wife Elizabeth and their two eldest children, Fanny and Edward (three younger boys, George, Henry and William, were left behind in Kent), he left Godmersham and travelled to Bath, stopping off at Steventon to pick up his mother and younger sister on the way.

The Austen party rented a house at 13 Queen Square for six weeks in May and June. The *Bath Chronicle*, which each week announced the latest prominent people to arrive in the city, recorded in its issue of Thursday 23 May 1799 the arrival of a 'Mr and Mrs E Austin' [*sic*].[2] Presumably, Miss J. Austen, as their poor relation, did not merit a mention. As soon as she was over the threshold of the house in Queen Square she sat down to write to Cassandra: 'Well, here we are at Bath; we got here at about one o'clock & have been arrived just long enough to go over the whole house, fix on our rooms, & be very well pleased with the whole of it.'

On the way to their lodgings the Austens had called in on Mr and Mrs Leigh Perrot in The Paragon, and, as was quite normal in Bath, had run into quite a few acquaintances on the way. I love Jane's description of one of these encounters: 'At the bottom of Kingsdown Hill we met a Gentleman in a Buggy, who on a minute examination turned out to be Dr Hall – and Dr Hall in such very deep mourning that either his Mother, his Wife or himself must be dead.' Jane's letter goes on to describe their accommodation in Queen Square and the landlady, a Mrs Bromley: '… the rooms are quite as large as we expected, Mrs Bromley is a fat woman in mourning & a little black kitten runs about the Staircase.'

Built in the Palladian style, Queen Square was among the first new developments in Bath to be designed by John Wood the Elder, one of the primary architects of Georgian Bath. On its completion in 1735 the square was the height of fashion, but by 1799, with all the newer developments that had been built to the north and east of Bath, it was no longer *the* place to stay. Jane Austen does not appear to have minded this: 'I like our situation very much – it is far more chearful [*sic*] than Paragon.' Mrs Austen agreed: a couple of years later in January 1801, when the Austens were house-hunting ahead of their move to Bath, Jane wrote: 'My mother hankers after the Square dreadfully.' This did not prevent Jane from being satirically aware of the signals that the location of one's lodgings sent out. In *Persuasion* the Misses Musgrove remark: 'I hope we shall be in Bath in the winter; but remember, Papa, if we do go, we must be in a good situation – none of your Queen Squares for us!'

We drove round Queen Square on the open-top bus. The top deck afforded a good view of the obelisk in the middle, erected in memory of Frederick, Prince of Wales, the eldest son of George II, who died in 1751 after being hit by a tennis ball – or so the apocryphal story, perpetuated by the bus commentary, goes. In fact, a burst abscess in the lung was given as the official cause of death. It was thus Frederick's son who acceded to the throne in 1760 as George III. As the bus commentary remarked, for the benefit of passengers from across the pond, he was to be the 'last king of the US'. Queen Square was also home to the renowned Dr William Oliver, who lived in a house on the west side. When he died in 1764 he is said to have bequeathed the recipe for the famous Bath Oliver biscuit to his coachman Atkins, together with a sack of flour and some money. Atkins set up in business to make the biscuits and became rich. You can still buy them of course, although they are no longer made in Bath.

Later I walked round the square on foot. It's certainly an elegant place to live, and convenient for all that Bath has to offer, especially the shops. It's a stone's throw to the back door of Jolly's department store on Milsom Street, with its designer fashions, for example. Jolly's wasn't here in Jane Austen's time, but dates back to 1830. Bath has always been famed for its shopping. As Mrs Allen remarks to Henry Tilney in *Northanger Abbey*: 'there are so many good shops here... one can step out of doors and get a thing in five minutes.' Jane herself describes lots of shopping trips in her letters, although she was not always tempted to buy: 'I saw some gauzes in a shop in Bath Street yesterday at only 4s [four shillings] a yard, but they were not so good or so pretty as mine', she wrote in June 1799. Queen square is evidently still a desirable place to live: a Grade I listed two-bedroom 'apartment' on the square, with no outside space, was on the market with the estate agents Hamptons for £325,000. Like much of Bath today, however, it is plagued by heavy traffic. At the time of my visit the *Bath Chronicle* was reporting on the 'Dirty Dozen' streets in the city, including nearby Gay Street, that are 'choked by dangerous pollutants'.

Despite the absence of exhaust fumes in the 18th century, it's not clear whether Edward Austen's stay in Bath in the late Spring of 1799 had a beneficial effect on his health or not. He regularly took the waters of the Hot Bath at the Hetling Pump Room and Jane reported to Cassandra after three weeks or so that: 'Edward has been pretty well for this last week, and as the waters have never disagreed with him in any respect, we are inclined to hope that he will derive advantage from them in the end.' A week later, however, she wrote that he has 'not been well these last two days; his appetite has failed him, & he has complained of sick and uncomfortable feelings, which with other symptoms make us think of the Gout.' An apothecary he consulted later attributed the problem to 'his having ate something unsuited to his stomach'. His ailments did not prevent Edward from buying a new pair of coach horses before he left Bath. His younger sister was back in Steventon by the end of June 1799.

After my freezing bus trip I decided on a brisk uphill walk and headed up the raised pavements of The Paragon, past the house where Jane Austen's aunt and uncle, Mr and Mrs Leigh Perrot, once lived. Today it has an unloved air, and its windows are shuttered and dirty. Its condition is somehow appropriate. Jane reported that when the Leigh Perrots returned there for the Bath season in early 1809 they 'found their House so dirty & so damp that they were obliged to be a week at an Inn.'

The renowned tragic actress Sarah Siddons lived at no. 33 The Paragon for a number of years during the 1770s and 1780s. She enjoyed huge success playing Lady Macbeth to packed houses at the Theatre Royal in Bath and in *The School for Scandal* by Sheridan. In 1782 she left for London, having been invited to perform at Drury Lane by the new manager there, who was none other than Sheridan himself. In 1811, while she was staying in London with her brother Henry, a keen theatre-goer, Jane wrote to Cassandra that she regretted that she had had 'no chance of seeing Mrs Siddons', her disappointment implying that she hadn't managed to see her in Bath either, despite her regular trips to the theatre there.

It was at no. 1 The Paragon that Jane Austen stayed with the Leigh Perrots when she and her mother arrived in Bath in May 1801, to go house-hunting. In early January Jane discussed the pros and cons of various locations in the city in a letter to Cassandra: 'We know that Mrs Perrot will want to get us into Axford Buildings, but we all unite in particular dislike of that part of the Town & therefore hope to escape.' Axford Buildings was very close to The Paragon and it is clear that Jane did not always get on with her aunt. 'I flatter myself that our apartment will be one of the most complete things of the sort all over Bath – Bristol included', she adds cheerfully. The winter season was over, which must have increased the number of properties on offer. 'Bath is getting so very empty that I am not afraid of doing too little', Jane wrote to Cassandra. Still, her letters detail a busy round of parties and social gatherings throughout the month of May, as the search for a suitable house continued. Cassandra and her father joined them in Bath shortly afterwards.

Then there is a three-year silence. No more letters survive until September 1804, when Jane wrote to Cassandra while on holiday at Lyme Regis. Despite the lack of letters, we know that the Austens eventually decided on a house across Pulteney Bridge at 4 Sydney Place. On 21 May 1801 an advertisement appeared in the Bath Chronicle for a lease of three and a quarter years on the property: 'The situation is desirable, the Rent very low and the Landlord is bound by Contract to paint the first two floors this summer.'[3] Having taken the house, the Austens took themselves off on holiday to Sidmouth in Devon to allow the redecoration to take place.

I walked up Walcot Street and peered into the windows of some of its many antique shops. At the top of the street, at a busy road junction, is St Swithin's Church, where Jane's parents were married and where her father lies buried. There is a curious synergy at work here, as St Swithin is also the patron saint of Winchester Cathedral, where Jane Austen herself is buried. St Swithin's in Bath, with its landmark classical spire, is the city's only surviving Georgian parish church. The Austens are not the only notables to be associated with the church – William Wilberforce also got married here and, next to a stone commemorating the death of George Austen in a lawned area to the north of the church, there is a cenotaph to Le Comte D'Arblay, the husband of the novelist Fanny Burney, whose work Jane read and admired. The church was undergoing restoration work and was surrounded by steel grilles. In the small churchyard George Austen's memorial tablet was shrouded in bright orange netting. What with the sound of hammering and chiselling, and the noise of the traffic zooming right past its doors, it was hard to imagine a less tranquil place.

Finally, after another steep climb, I found myself in Camden Crescent, at the very top of Georgian Bath. The houses here enjoy panoramic views of the city and the grandeur of the crescent's distinctive shape is visible from many vantage points below. It is in Camden Crescent, known to Jane Austen as Camden-place, that Anne Elliot's snobbish father, Sir Walter Elliot, stays when he comes to Bath: 'Sir Walter had taken a very good house in Camden-place – a lofty distinguished situation, such as becomes a man of consequence; and both he and Elizabeth were settled there, much to their satisfaction.' The Elliots, mired in the debts racked up through Sir Walter's imprudence, have come to Bath to save money, having rented out the family seat, Kellynch-hall, to Admiral Croft and his wife, sister to Anne's former love, Captain Wentworth. The business of economizing is, however, alien to Sir Walter and his eldest daughter: 'Their house was undoubtedly the best in Camden-place; their drawing rooms had many decided advantages over all the others which they had either seen or heard of; and the superiority was not less in the style of the fitting-up, or the taste of the furniture.' Perhaps Jane had in mind for them the grandest house in the crescent, which is topped with a large decorative pediment.

Jane Austen was adept at choosing locations to suit her characters. This is particularly true of the Bath addresses she selects in *Persuasion*, which has snobbery as one of its prevailing themes. Anne Elliot's old school-friend Mrs Smith, who is crippled with rheumatic fever, lodges in a 'very humble way' in Westgate Buildings, in the lower part of the city, within carrying distance of the Cross Bath. Sir Walter is most put out when he discovers that Anne is deigning to frequent such a place, and to visit a mere Smith at that: 'Westgate Buildings! … and who is a Miss Anne Elliot to be visiting in Westgate Buildings? A Mrs Smith! Westgate Buildings must have been rather surprised by the appearance of a carriage drawn up near its pavement.' On a later visit, there is no lift in Lady Russell's carriage, so Anne must make the long downhill walk from Camden Place to Westgate Buildings. She doesn't mind because it gives her the opportunity to muse on 'high-wrought love and eternal constancy'. The uphill trek back is less pleasant: after a visit to the Musgroves, who are staying in the lower part of town, Anne is faced with 'a toilsome walk to Camden-place'. It's a grand address, but one that implies the use of a carriage at all times, a privilege that Anne Elliot does not enjoy.

There's an even better reason why elevated Camden Crescent is an inspired choice of residence for vain Sir Walter. The crescent, begun around 1788, was actually supposed to form part of a much larger development, but a series of serious landslips, common at that time in this part of the city, brought work to a permanent halt with only part of the crescent completed. Its central pediment is off-centre to this day, as originally another four houses were to have been added at the far end. Jane Austen, quite intentionally it seems, placed Sir Walter on shaky ground.

I crossed the road and sat on a bench by a bus stop, looking down across the city, and trying not to notice the cast-off traffic cones and road signs dumped on the slopes below. There was a smell of smoke, which told me fires were being laid indoors. Though it was still only mid-afternoon, the dusk was closing in. Time to move on, time for tea.

Back down in Gay Street, close to Queen Square, a diminutive dummy in a blue bonnet and an embroidered 'Open' sign usher visitors into the Georgian townhouse that is the Jane Austen Centre. It's an appropriate location: Jane Austen herself lived in the same street for a time, although not in this house. Happily even Sir Walter Elliot would deem it quite an acceptable address: in *Persuasion* Admiral and Mrs Croft place themselves in lodgings in Gay Street 'perfectly to his satisfaction'. In the front room I bought a ticket for the last tour of the day and headed gratefully upstairs to the second floor tearooms, which were as chintzy and as genteel as any Jane Austen devotee could wish for: Wedgwood blue walls, toile de Jouy curtains and a budding daffodil on every table. I had no problem deciding on a pot of 'Jane Austen' tea ('a blend of China black teas popular in Regency times'), but had to deliberate for some time over the victuals. On offer were 'Cassandra's Coffee and Walnut Cake', 'Darcy's Crumble', 'Willoughby's Chocolate Fudge Cake' (wicked, obviously), 'Mrs Bennet's Moist Sponge Loaf', 'Cousin Collins' Crumpets' (Mr Collins? Crumpet?) and 'Emma's English Muffins'. Eventually I opted for 'Lady Catherine's Proper Cream Tea'. ('Obstinate, headstrong girl!', as Lady Catherine herself might have put it). It was very tempting to play at creating additional dishes of one's own – Miss De Bourgh's dry toast, perhaps? Or maybe Mr Rushworth's Gooseberry Fool?

I made myself stop making fun of the menu. Everything was delicious, and the service was friendly and smiling. I drank several cups of tea and then it was time for my tour. Licking the last of the cream from my lips, I went down to a first-floor room that displays letters from such eminent fans of Jane Austen as

John Major and Jeffrey Archer, complimenting the Centre on its displays. Our guide arrived promptly, and we filed into the next-door room to listen to a short talk about Jane Austen and Bath. It gave a lot of prominence to Jane's probable and possible suitors – Tom Lefroy, Harris Bigg-Wither and the gentlemen to whom she is supposed to have become close in Devon. 'Jane Austen was too much of a romantic to marry for economic reasons', said the guide. She was no romantic, I thought rebelliously in my back-row seat. She just wanted to be free to write.

I stayed the night in a beautiful Georgian guesthouse on the southern slopes of Bath, close to Beechen Cliff. My host and his partner welcomed me very warmly, and invited me for a glass of red wine and then for supper. The conversation turned to the eldest of my host's three teenagers, who at 19 he felt, was a little too young to be getting so serious about his girlfriend. Though our lovely period surroundings had more than a whiff of Jane Austen's time, this was a dilemma of the modern era, light years away from a time when, at 19, many women were already married with children. Then we talked about marriage and the difficulties of finding the right partner, and how money – both a lack of it and a generous supply – has a tendency to complicate things. Suddenly we were right back in the 18th century.

Of course, women today have the luxury of being far more romantic about love and marriage than they did in Jane Austen's time. Most women then, particularly those without independent means, were expected to take a pragmatic view of the estate and get themselves off the shelf before their time ran out. Anne

Elliot, still a spinster at the age of 27, has sacrificed a great deal
by staying faithful to the only man she has ever loved, Captain
Wentworth: 'Her attachment and regrets, had for a long time,
clouded every enjoyment of youth; and an early loss of bloom
and spirits had been their lasting effect.'

Jane Austen also made a sacrifice, not for the love of her life,
but, I had begun to believe, for her work. In 1802 Jane left Bath
with Cassandra on a visit to their childhood friends Elizabeth,
Alethea and Catherine Bigg at Manydown House near
Basingstoke. During their stay the Bigg sisters' younger brother,
Harris, proposed to Jane. She accepted him and the whole
household went to bed rejoicing at the match. The next morning, after a sleepless night, Jane decided that she had made a
mistake and declined his proposal. She and Cassandra left
Manydown under a cloud, and returned to Bath.

Harris Bigg-Wither was the heir to a considerable estate. If she
had married him, Jane, at 27, would have been mistress of a
large Hampshire house close to her birthplace, and could have
assured the comfort of her parents and her sister for the rest of
their lives. This makes it more understandable, perhaps, that she
succumbed to temptation, if only for one night. Of course she
did not love Harris Bigg-Wither, but this was not an insur-
mountable hurdle. After all, another 27-year-old, Charlotte
Lucas, had embraced a worse fate in engaging herself to Mr
Collins in *Pride and Prejudice*: 'I am not romantic you know. I
never was. I ask only a comfortable home.' Surely what Jane
Austen could not bear to give up was the freedom to write. For
this she was prepared to forsake what was probably her last
chance of a suitable marriage. Let us give thanks for that sleepless night. As Claire Tomalin puts it: 'We would naturally rather

have *Mansfield Park* and *Emma* than the Bigg-Wither baby Jane Austen might have given the world, and who would almost certainly have prevented her from writing any further books.'⁴ But what would Jane have done had she met a Captain Wentworth?

Despite my very comfortable lodgings, I spent a disturbed night myself, notions of love and marriage, and what they have to do with each other, going round in my head until the early hours.

The next morning, after breakfast, I followed a footpath across a muddy field, full of cows and thistles, to Beechen Cliff. It was misty and Sunday morning church bells were ringing out across the city below. Here on this 'noble hill, whose beautiful verdure and hanging coppice render it so striking an object from almost every opening in Bath', Catherine Morland comes for a walk with Henry Tilney and his sister in *Northanger Abbey*. A lengthy discussion ensues about their preferred reading material. Catherine Morland, at 17, is already in love with Mr Tilney. Jane Austen signals her approval of her heroine's choice, as she so often does, by revealing that Tilney is a reader: 'The person, be it gentleman or lady, who has not pleasure in a good novel must be intolerably stupid', he says. Tilney is also a bit of a one for playing with the English language. He teases Catherine mercilessly for her choice of words. When she calls *The Mysteries of Udolpho* a 'nice book' he replies: 'Very true… and this is a very nice day, and we are taking a very nice walk, and you are two very nice young ladies. Oh! Not? It is a very nice word indeed! – it does for every thing.'

At their first meeting, in the Lower Rooms, Tilney remarks to Catherine that 'nothing in the world advances intimacy so much' as teasing. So it proves, for Tilney and Catherine Morland are married 'within a twelvemonth of the first day of their meeting'. You only tease people you like, after all, although I didn't always manage to take comfort from this fact when I first met my own husband. When he introduced me to his closest friends, their camaraderie forged back in their Surrey primary school days, they teased me to such an extent that it became almost an initiation rite. Oddly enough, the way I said 'Bath', with my short East Midlands 'a', exposed me to particularly intense ribbing.

In the company of dog-walkers I had a very 'nice' walk on Beechen Cliff, enjoying the views to Bath Abbey and Camden Crescent beyond, just visible through the mist. This is exactly the view that prompts the Tilneys to a discussion about whether it qualifies as 'picturesque' (it does not). Catherine, ashamed of her ignorance of such matters, is all ears: 'Catherine was so hopeful a scholar that when they gained the top of Beechen Cliff, she voluntarily rejected the whole city of Bath, as unworthy to make part of a landscape.'

It's a blissfully funny and ironic passage. Jane Austen as narrator appears to support her heroine in her ignorance by commenting: 'When people wish to attach, they should always be ignorant. To come with a well-informed mind is to come with an inability of administering to the vanity of others, which a sensible person would always wish to avoid. A woman, especially, if she have the misfortune of knowing any thing, should conceal it as well as she can.' How fortunate it is that Jane herself was singularly incapable of following such advice. She knew only too well that people are vain and that many men find clever women difficult. Perhaps the fact that Jane Austen encountered few men who felt that they could attach themselves to her owes something to the fact that she was so singularly incapable of appearing ignorant.

This passage in *Northanger Abbey* reminds us how dangerous it is to assume that the opinions expressed in her novels are those of the author herself. Yet almost every writer on Jane Austen has been lured into such assumptions, particularly when her feelings about Bath are under scrutiny. In *Persuasion* Anne Elliot, who spent three years at school in Bath after the death of her mother, is no fan of the place: 'She disliked Bath and did not think it agreed with her.' Little wonder then that, when she arrives for what is to be a lengthy stay, 'she caught the first dim view of the extensive buildings, smoking in rain, without any wish of seeing them better.' This no more reflects Jane Austen's own feelings than the passage in *Northanger Abbey* that describes Catherine Morland's very different state of mind on getting her own first glimpse of the place: 'Catherine was all eager delight; – her eyes were here, there, every where, as they approached its fine and striking environs, and afterwards drove through those streets which conducted them to the hotel. She was come to be happy, and she felt happy already.' And later: 'Oh! who can ever be tired of Bath?'

I've fallen into the trap myself. After I read *Love and Freindship* it was clear to me that Jane Austen could not possibly ever have fainted, but what did she really think of Bath? It seems more legitimate to look for evidence of Jane's feelings in her own letters, but even this approach has its pitfalls. When she arrived with her mother to begin the search for a permanent home in May 1801, Jane wrote to Cassandra: 'The first veiw [*sic*] in fine weather does not answer my expectations; I think I see more distinctly thro' Rain. – The Sun was got behind everything, and the appearance of the place from the top of Kingsdown Hill was all vapour, shadow, smoke and confusion.' This comment is regularly cited as evidence of Jane's dislike of Bath, yet all she actually admits is that her first sight of the place was a bit hazy. Views can be confusing things. After Henry Tilney's lecture on the picturesque, Catherine Morland leaves Beechen Cliff having had her own opinions on views, such as they were, turned upside down: 'It seemed as if a good view were no longer to be taken from the top of an high hill, and that a clear blue sky was no longer a proof of a fine day.'

It was too cold to linger on Beechen Cliff. Down in the city once more, I parked my cold bones by a window in a café under Pulteney Bridge and looked out at the River Avon, its bottle-green waters rippling like rickrack as they slipped towards the weir. A succession of logs and large branches had become caught, and were suspended above its foaming rapids, one large log looking uncannily like a crocodile. A swan glided by, dipping its beak unconcernedly in the weedy shallows. At the next table a couple of young Bath bucks demolished a restorative morning-after-the-night-before breakfast. But for the mobile phones and the i-Mac open on the table, they could have been James Morland and John Thorpe of *Northanger Abbey*. John Thorpe would be the more hung-over-looking of the two: 'There is no drinking at Oxford I assure you... it was reckoned a remarkable thing at the last party in my rooms, that upon an average we cleared about five pints a head.' Across the room a small boy drummed his heels as his father struggled to release a newly bought toy fire engine from some fiendish packaging.

Fortified by good coffee, I strolled across Pulteney Bridge to the newest part of 18th-century Bath, built on Sir William Pulteney's former Bathwick estate. Once the Bathwick side had been connected to the rest of Bath with the completion of Robert Adam's bridge, in 1774, various plans for the estate were prepared. A scheme by Thomas Baldwin, incorporating wide new avenues and crescents, and elegant side streets, was eventually adopted. Work began in 1788, but before long the turmoil and financial panic that followed the events of 1789 in Paris led to the collapse of the bank that had provided the funds for the development. Baldwin went bankrupt and building work ground to a halt, leaving a great deal unfinished, including Sunderland Street, which to this day is only one house long on each side. The open-top bus commentary had made a joke of it, dubbing it the Bath postie's favourite street.

Unfinished though it may be, this is still one of the most beautiful and impressive parts of Georgian Bath. Great Pulteney Street, which leads from Pulteney Bridge to Sydney Gardens at its eastern end, is 1,000 feet long and more than 100 feet wide, a magnificent and stately thoroughfare unrivalled in grandeur anywhere else in the city. Accordingly, some of Bath's most distinguished visitors and residents have stayed here, their presences recorded by the succession of plaques that you can see as you walk along the street: Admiral Earl Howe, Prince Louis-Napoleon (later Emperor Napoleon III), William Wilberforce, Hannah More (another notable opponent of the slave trade). Another plaque denotes the house where William Smith, the 'father of English Geology', dictated *The Order of the Strata* in December 1799.

It is in 'Pulteney-street' that the Allens find 'comfortable lodgings' in *Northanger Abbey* when they bring Catherine Morland to Bath. Despite the cars that now permanently line both sides of the street, it is easy to imagine them emerging from between the Corinthian columns of a house here. Most are smartly kept, with pots of bay or box on their front steps, but the majority have long since been divided into flats or converted into accountants' offices or doctors' surgeries. One retains swagged curtains and even a sedan chair outside, but this is a hotel, beloved of American visitors.

The curtains are a reminder of the incident in *Persuasion* when Anne Elliot spies Captain Wentworth walking down the right-hand pavement of Pulteney-street while she is out driving in Lady Russell's carriage. She is sure that Lady Russell, the woman who has persuaded Anne to break off her engagement, has fixed her eye on him too, but it turns out that she is actually looking for some drawing-room curtains reputed to be 'the handsomest and best hung of any in Bath'. A more recent fixture on the pavement is an ornate hexagonal pillarbox, stamped 'VR'. Its slot was bound with tape and covered with a handwritten yellow sign reading 'Post Box Out of Service'. In revenge someone had scrawled 'Bum Office' in black pen on its elegant scrolled top.

I turned with some excitement into Sydney Place, Jane's home from 1801 to 1805. Despite the beckoning tranquillity of Sydney Gardens across the road, no. 4 Sydney Place is another traffic-choked milestone on the Jane Austen trail. Cars and lorries zoom past its door on their way to the M4. I narrowly missed being run over by a bus, which swung around the corner as I crossed to take a photograph from the other side of the road.

While researching *Jane Austen: Her Homes and Her Friends* a hundred years ago, Constance Hill managed to gain entrance. She found a 'roomy and commodious house', sat in its 'pretty drawing room with three tall windows overlooking the gardens', and peered into a 'large old-fashioned kitchen with its shining copper pans, and its dresser laden with fine old china'.[5] Today the four-storey house has peeling paintwork, but someone apparently cares for it, because the brass had been polished and a window box was planted with narcissi. A plaque reads simply: 'Here lived Jane Austen, 1801–05'. Inexplicably I found myself staring at the bootscraper by the front door. Was it original? Should I scrape my own boots there in homage, just in case?

Back across Pulteney Bridge again, I met Roger near the Pump Rooms. Roger was to be my official guide on the Jane Austen Centre Walking Tour of Bath. Unfortunately for him, on this cold Sunday in February I was his only customer. I lost no time in challenging him: 'So Jane Austen disliked Bath, did she? What makes you think that?' Roger took my sparring in good humour and claimed to like it when someone knew a bit about his subject.

His tour wended enjoyably in the tracks of Jane Austen's characters. We walked through the Pump Yard to the archway opposite Union-passage, as Catherine Morland and Isabella Thorpe do in *Northanger Abbey*, and imagined their difficulties in crossing Cheap Street. At that time it was 'a street of so impertinent a nature, so unfortunately connected with the great London and Oxford Roads'. Through the chaos of arriving carriages the two ladies spot their respective brothers, James Morland and the boorish 'rattle' John Thorpe, who have just arrived in Bath. Thorpe boasts at length about the speed and prowess of his poor horses ('nothing ruins horses so much as rest') in exactly the same way as certain men are wont to drone on about their cars today.

Roger then led the way to the site of the White Hart Inn in Stall Street. The White Hart was, in Jane Austen's day, the principal coaching inn of Bath. In *Persuasion* it is here that the Musgroves take rooms overlooking the entrance to the Pump Rooms. When Mary Musgrove looks out of the window, she is startled to see Mrs Clay standing 'deep in talk' with the villainous Mr Elliot under the colonnade, close to the entrance to the Pump Room (later we learn that Mrs Clay is 'established under his protection' in London).

It is also at the White Hart that the miraculous denouement of the novel takes place, when Captain Wentworth hands Anne a letter confessing his enduring love for her. The final two chapters of the novel caused Jane Austen some problems. In the first ending she wrote, Anne Elliot and Captain Wentworth are reunited at the Gay Street lodgings of the Crofts. When they are left alone for a moment Captain Wentworth tells Anne that he has heard she is to marry Mr Elliot. When Anne denies it he immediately proposes to her. Yet Jane soon realized the flaw: what makes Captain Wentworth so sure that Anne still cares for him? In 1816, when she was already suffering from the illness that eventually killed her, Jane reworked the final two chapters. The discarded chapters are the only piece of manuscript from her finished novels to survive: they are now in the British Library and, of course, are incredibly precious. However, the ending we know and love today is much more satisfying, as

Anne's overheard remarks to Captain Harville are the catalyst for their renewed engagement. 'All the privilege I claim for my own sex', cries Anne, 'is that of loving longest, when existence or when hope is gone.' 'I can no longer listen in silence', writes Captain Wentworth. 'You pierce my soul.'

Today, the White Hart is long gone and on the site today stand three temples of modern retail: an O2 mobile phone shop, a branch of Bhs and the Edinburgh Woollen Mill. Roger pointed out the site of Smith's nearby, a now empty shop on the corner of Bath Street from which Jane's aunt, Mrs Leigh Perrot, was accused of stealing a length of white lace (she was put on trial but was acquitted).

Further on, in Milsom Street, we stopped to pay homage at no. 2, formerly Molland's the pastry-cook shop, where Anne Elliot shelters from the rain with her sister and Mrs Clay. From the window she sees Captain Wentworth walking down the street with a new umbrella with which he has 'equipped himself properly for Bath'. In *Northanger Abbey* Isabella Thorpe twitters on to Catherine about 'the prettiest hat' she has seen in a shop-window in Milsom Street: 'very like yours, only with coquelicot ribbons instead of green'.

I was particularly keen to see Bond Street – now Old Bond Street. Here the conceited Sir Walter Elliot stands in a shop and counts 'eighty-seven women go by, one after another, without there being a tolerable face among them'. This prompts him to a diatribe on the 'multitude of ugly women in Bath': 'He did not mean to say that there were no pretty women, but the number of the plain was out of all proportion. He had frequently observed as he walked, that one handsome face would be followed by thirty, or five and thirty frights.'

We left the shopping streets behind us and walked, via Queen Square, to The Circus, a glorious circle of houses modelled on the Colosseum in Rome and built in 1754 by John Wood the Elder. Houses in the Circus apparently had the luxury of Bath's first piped water supply. The story goes that people in lower Bath were so jealous that they polluted the water. Illustrious residents of the Circus have included Lord Clive of Plassey ('Clive of India'), David Livingstone, Thomas Gainsborough and Major John André, hanged as a spy during the American War of Independence. The combination of America and circuses reminded me of an amusing story I'd heard at dinner the previous evening. An American visitor who was planning a visit to London had apparently phoned the British Tourism Office in New York to ask what time the Piccadilly Circus began.

Roger and I proceeded from the Circus to the Royal Crescent, begun in 1775, the year of Jane Austen's birth, and known on completion simply as The Crescent. During the season this was the place to parade on a Sunday morning after church, particularly in fine weather. In *Northanger Abbey* we are told that 'a fine Sunday in Bath empties every house of its inhabitants, and all the world appears on such an occasion to walk about and tell their acquaintance what a charming day it is.' Having found 'not a genteel face to be seen' in the crowded Pump Rooms, the Thorpes and the Allens 'hasten away to the Crescent to breath the fresh air of better company'. Jane Austen certainly came here. In a letter of 8 April 1805 she wrote: 'We did not walk long in the Crescent yesterday, it was hot and not crouded enough.'

The grand houses in the Crescent once looked out across fields of grazing livestock. Now the view is of the Royal Victoria Park, opened by the 11-year-old Princess Victoria in 1830.

According to the open-top bus commentary the day before, a local Bath newspaper had reported on the occasion and described her as looking dowdy. The Princess had taken offence and refused to visit Bath ever again. When, in 1899, the octogenarian Queen Victoria was forced to pass through the city on Brunel's Great Western Railway, she apparently still bore the grudge, for she ordered that the blinds on the train be lowered.

We left the Crescent and walked down the Gravel Walk, a secluded pedestrian thoroughfare designed by John Wood the Younger to link Queen Square with The Crescent. Here Anne Elliot and Captain Wentworth, their engagement renewed, 'slowly paced the gradual ascent, heedless of every group around them, seeing neither sauntering politicians, bustling house-keepers, flirting girls, nor nursery-maids and children'. Roger and I looked in vain for politicians and flirtatious girls, though there were plenty of families with the sort of very young children whose morning energies demand fresh air and exercise. There were also a few joggers intent on the same.

Roger's tour ended at the door of the Assembly Rooms. As we said goodbye, we decided to agree to differ over the issue of whether Jane Austen had really liked Bath or not. I apologized for trying to tempt him into departing from the accepted tourist guide script and hoped that he would soon be chaperoning some less argumentative visitors.

The Assembly Rooms were known in Jane Austen's time as the New Rooms or the Upper Rooms. This was to distinguish them from the Lower Rooms, another venue for assemblies, which once stood between Bath Abbey and the river. According to a definition of 1751, an assembly was 'a stated and general meeting of the polite persons of both sexes, for the sake of conversation, gallantry, news and play'. The Lower Rooms, which were built much earlier, in around 1708, were destroyed by fire in 1820. It is at the Lower Rooms that Catherine Morland is first introduced to Henry Tilney, 'a very gentlemanlike man', by Mr King, the Master of Ceremonies. A Mr King was indeed the Master of Ceremonies here in the 1790s. Mr Tilney, possibly my favourite of Austen's heroes for his witty way with words, gently mocks Catherine as they dance by telling her he knows exactly how she will record their encounter in her diary the following day: 'Friday, went to the Lower Rooms; wore my sprigged muslin robe with blue trimmings – plain black shoes – appeared to much advantage; but was strangely harassed by a queer, half-witted man, who would make me dance with him, and distressed me by his nonsense.'

By the late 18th century the 'fashionable centre of gravity', as Maggie Lane calls it,[6] had shifted as Bath expanded northwards, establishing the most desirable addresses in the upper part of town. It was a very long way home from the Lower Rooms by sedan chair for those residing in Camden Place or in the vicinity of The Crescent. Consequently, that venue lost much of its glamour after the opening of the Upper Rooms in 1771. These magnificent new Rooms were designed by John Wood the Younger and purpose-built for assemblies on a site close to The Circus, at a cost of £14,000, raised by shareholders. Badly damaged by an air raid during the Second World War, they have now been restored to their former glory. The basement houses Bath's Museum of Costume, but I decided to forgo the frocks in favour of the Rooms, which are the setting for some memorable scenes in Jane Austen's two Bath novels.

Patrons entered the Rooms through an octagonal foyer and proceeded through to the yellow Octagon or Card Room, off which all the other rooms lead. During the evening assemblies this area was packed with card-players engaged in gambling away their fortunes. On Sundays, when gambling was not allowed, organ recitals were held instead. Today the room is still presided over by portraits of King George III and Queen Charlotte, together with a painting from the studio of another Bath resident, Thomas Gainsborough, of Captain William Wade, the first Master of Ceremonies of the Assembly Rooms, wearing his blue badge of office. The sparkling chandelier that now hangs weightily over visitors is not the original, but was made from one of the original ballroom chandeliers, an arm of which fell off only a month after the Rooms first opened, narrowly missing Captain Wade. There are four fireplaces, necessary to counter the cold of the winter season: the high ceilings ensured that there was also plenty of ventilation. In *Persuasion* it is next to one of these fires that the Elliots 'station' themselves as they await the arrival of the Dowager Viscountess Dalrymple, who 'must be waited for' (Lady Dalrymple, a distant Irish cousin, is one of the very few people in Bath to whom Sir Walter Elliot will defer). After snatching a short conversation with Captain Wentworth, Anne appears positively radiant, but her feelings are later thrown into confusion during the concert they are attending when she realizes that her former fiancé is jealous of the attentions paid to her by Mr Elliot: 'How was such jealousy to be quieted?... How in all the peculiar disadvantages of their respective situations would he ever learn her real sentiments?'

Next door to the Octagon Room is the spectacular blue-green Ballroom, with its richly stuccoed ceiling. It's like being on the inside of an immense wedding cake, its interior encrusted with royal icing. This huge room, nearly 107 feet long by 44 feet wide, could accommodate up to 1,000 guests at the twice weekly balls and frequent concerts. Windows surround three sides, at a high level to ensure the guests' privacy. The upper walls boast huge Corinthian columns and from the ceiling hang five staggering chandeliers made in London of Whitefriars crystal with razor-sharp icicle- and diamond-shaped droplets. When all five were lit by hundreds of beeswax candles it must have been a mesmerizing sight. The spectacle was not without its hazards, however: the candles were wont to wilt and drop hot wax onto the revellers below.

Balls followed a strict and accepted timetable. They began at 6 p.m. sharp with a stately minuet. At 8 p.m. more energetic country dances took over and at 9 p.m. refreshments were served in the Tea Room, which was situated back through the Octagon Room. Consequently, the players, intent on their card games, were often fatally distracted by the comings and goings, so much so that a new Card Room was later added. After tea the fun continued in the ballroom until the orchestra stopped playing on the very stroke of 11, even in the middle of a dance.

I sat for quite some time, trying to conjure up the crush described in *Northanger Abbey* in my mind's eye, but I was somewhat handicapped by the fact that I was the only person in an empty room. In *Northanger Abbey* preparations for Catherine Morland's first ball take several days, since Catherine's 'entrée into life could not take place till after three or four days had

been spent in learning what was mostly worn', and until she
is 'provided with a dress of the newest fashion' by Mrs Allen.
On the day of the auspicious event itself her hair is 'cut and
dressed by the best hand, her clothes put on with care, and Mrs
Allen and her maid declared she looked quite as she should do.'
When the Allens arrive, the season is full, the room crowded,
and the two ladies have to squeeze in as well as they can, while
Mr Allen repairs directly to the card room, leaving them to
'enjoy a mob by themselves'. The ladies push their way through
the crowd to the top of the room, hoping to find seats from
which they can watch the dancing, but the throng is still such
that they see 'nothing of the dancers but the high feathers of
some of the ladies' (headdresses with tall feathers were then all
the rage).

Jane Austen herself must have attended many such evenings,
though only one account survives among her letters, that of a
ball she went to with her Uncle and Aunt Leigh Perrot in May
1801. On that occasion there was no difficulty whatsoever in
locating the dancers: 'By nine o'clock, my Uncle, Aunt and I
entered the rooms & linked Miss Winstone on to us. – Before
tea, it was rather a dull affair; but then the beforetea (sic) did not
last long, for there was only one dance, danced by four couple.
– Think of four couple, surrounded by about an hundred people, dancing in the upper rooms at Bath!' The thinness of the
crowd was partly due to its being the end of the season, but, at
least among the most fashionable, attendance at the Rooms had
by this time given way to a preference for holding soirées at
home. After tea Jane and her companions cheered up considerably, as 'the breaking up of private Parties sent some scores more
to the Ball, and tho' it was shockingly & inhumanely thin for

this place, there were people enough I suppose to have made five or six very pretty Basingstoke assemblies'.

In the years that followed, the Assembly Rooms did not entirely lose their glamour and they were to make at least one more starring appearance in literature. In Charles Dickens's *The Pickwick Papers,* the Master of Ceremonies of the Rooms, the gloriously named Angelo Cyrus Bantam, Esq., tells Mr Pickwick on his arrival in Bath that 'The ball-nights in Ba-ath are moments snatched from Paradise; rendered bewitching by music, beauty, elegance, fashion, etiquette and – and – above all, by the absence of tradespeople who are quite inconsistent with Paradise.' Mr Pickwick duly attends a ball, at which the company 'pours in, in shoals'. Like Jane Austen before him, Dickens has great fun satirizing the foolish behaviour on display from such pillars of Bath society as the Dowager Lady Snuphanuph, Young Lord Mutanhed and Mrs Colonel Wugsby.

I had, not tea, but lunch in the Tea Room, which for a short period was hosting the restaurant normally housed at the Pump Rooms while the latter were closed for refurbishment. The Tea Room features three more huge chandeliers, adorned here and there with strands of cobweb (mind you, I wouldn't want the job of dusting them), and parlour palms in pots. A pianist entertained patrons with a medley of tunes on a Steinway Grand, including 'Let's Face the Music and Dance', whose lyrics speak of that heady cocktail of moonlight and love and romance that Catherine Morland hoped to find at the Assembly Rooms more than 200 years ago. The prismatic drops of the chandeliers transformed the winter sunshine into a rainbow light-show on the walls, and the parents of a small girl sitting at the next table twisted and turned their watches to catch the light and make what my Granny used to call a Jack O'Dandy dance for her. Another couple was celebrating something: at least they were once a red-faced waitress finally managed, after a good few minutes, to extract the cork from a bottle of champagne. I made some discreet notes, trying, like Jane Austen, to write very small on little bits of paper, which I slipped under my napkin when my food arrived.

Afterwards, in the shop, I pounced on a copy of that lecture entitled *Was Jane Austen Happy in Bath?*, given by the late Nigel Nicolson at the Holburne Museum of Art in Bath in 2002, in which he challenged the prevailing anti-Bath view:

> In assessing Jane Austen's reaction to Bath, it is important to be guided by her known character and likely response to these new circumstances. She was always alert for new experiences and a keen observer of human nature. She was a young woman who enjoyed life, and if things went wrong, she made the best of them.[7]

Roger should see this, I thought. Of course Jane had a good time in Bath. There were some dull moments – 'Another stupid party last night', she complains in one letter – but most of the time she seems to have been determined to enjoy herself, what with the walks and drives in the countryside, and the balls, concerts and theatre trips that are regularly mentioned in her letters.

One problem remains with the theory that Jane Austen's years in Bath were happy ones: while she was there she wrote very little. During her teenage and early adult years in Steventon she wrote almost constantly, but once she moved to Bath in 1801 she put down her pen. This, most biographers have surmised, was due to her unhappiness, or even depression, at being in the city. Carol Shields, to take a typical example, comments that: 'The silence asks questions about the flow of Jane Austen's creative energies, and about her reconciliation to the life she had been handed.'[8] Yet Jane Austen wrote even less in Southampton, where she lived between 1806 and 1809, and no one, it seems, has ever written about how much she disliked it there.

Perhaps Jane was too busy to write much in Bath, or maybe she lacked the seclusion she needed to match the output of previous years. Her mind was far from idle, however. Her revision in 1803 of *Susan*, the novel that she wrote around 1798 and that was to become *Northanger Abbey*, and the subsequent composition of *Persuasion* in 1815–16, show that her Bath years were far from wasted ones creatively.

What's more, Jane did start a new novel whilst in Bath. *The Watsons* puts the thorny subject of marriage under the spotlight as never before. Jane Austen began it in 1803 or 1804, not long after she had turned down Harris Bigg-Wither. When the novel opens, its heroine, Emma Watson, has just returned to the bosom of her genteel but poor family after many years away, during which time she has been brought up by a wealthy aunt. The aunt has remarried, depriving Emma of the generous inheritance she might once have hoped to have. Emma's rediscovered sister Elizabeth speaks movingly of her desperate need to find a husband: 'You know we must marry. – I could do very well single for my own part, – A little company and a pleasant ball now and then, would be enough for me, if one could be young forever, but my father cannot provide for us, and it is very bad to grow old and be poor and laughed at.'

The chequered business of finding and marrying the right man is something that all Jane Austen's novels have in common.

Jane sympathizes with Elizabeth Watson in her plight when she concludes: 'I think I could like any good humoured man with a comfortable income.' Even so, as she lay awake after accepting Harris Bigg-Wither's proposal, the thoughts going round and round Jane Austen's head were surely closer to those of Emma Watson, who declares: 'Poverty is a great evil, but to a woman of education and feeling it ought not, it cannot be the greatest.' Romantic? Not very.

The Austens spent three happy years at 4 Sydney Place, leaving the city each year to holiday on the south coast. By the time of their second stay at Lyme in 1804, however, the Austens had left their Sydney Place lodgings. Perhaps the rent proved too expensive. Their next home was at 3 Green Park Buildings East, close to the River Avon. When they had gone house-hunting in May 1801 they had viewed and dismissed a house in the same location. Despite its being 'so very desirable in size and situation', the 'observations of the damps', and 'reports of discontented families and putrid fevers', led the Austens to reject it. In 1804 something – probably lack of money – forced them to reconsider.

Two hundred years later there is no trace of the house. Much of this part of Georgian Bath was destroyed during German air raids conducted over two nights in April 1942. These attacks were among the 'Baedeker Raids', so called because the Nazis chose the targets for their cultural importance, selecting locations marked with three stars in the Baedeker travel guides. More than 100 bombers caused nearly 1,300 casualties and damaged 20,000 buildings. Today this part of Bath is a place of car parks, modern office blocks and beggars, who congregate close to the city's bus station. If Bath has an underbelly, this is probably it.

Within three months of their removal to Green Park Buildings Jane's father, the Reverend George Austen, was dead. He 'closed his virtuous and happy life', as Jane puts it, in January 1805, after two days' sudden illness. The lease on their lodgings had another three months to run, so his widow and daughters stayed until it was up. A few days later, Jane wrote from Green Park Buildings to her brother Frank, who was then at sea, and asked him to 'kindly press my Mother to remove to Steventon when it is all over', but it seems that Mrs Austen was in no hurry to leave Bath. Money was now a matter of grave concern, however. The greater part of the Reverend Austen's income was derived from his parish livings and terminated with his death, leaving his widow and daughters in greatly reduced circumstances. Jane's brothers rallied round and offered enough financial help to render them comfortable. Even so, their household expenditure had to be reduced. The Austens cut the number of servants they employed from three to one and were thus able to look for smaller lodgings. They found them at 25 Gay Street – a quite satisfactory location, as we have already seen – and had moved there by April 1805. Today 25 Gay Street is an attractive four-storey house, complete with cheerful window boxes to greet its 21st-century visitors, who come, not to drink tea and gossip, but to get their teeth filled at the dentist's surgery that it now houses.

The Austens were not long in Gay Street. Though none of Jane's letters from that address survives to explain why, they soon moved again, this time to Trim Street. In January 1801 Jane had written that her mother 'will do everything in her power to avoid Trim Street'. Four years later their reduced circumstances meant that they could avoid it no longer. Trim Street was cramped and narrow, and, unlike bustling Gay Street or elegant Sydney Gardens, it was tucked apologetically away from Bath's fashionable thoroughfares. Even today it feels like a comedown, worlds away from Queen Square just round the corner. Overloaded orange Biffa bins, spewing cardboard, sit outside the modern building that houses the Trim Street offices of Bath and North East Somerset Council.

Then, in 1806, Mrs Austen and her daughters were invited by Jane's brother Frank to live with him in Southampton. Frank, who had recently married, thought that his mother and sisters would be company for his wife Mary during his long absences at sea. It would also give everyone the opportunity to share expenses. The Austens left Bath for good on 1 July 1806 and, after making a round of visits to friends and relatives in Gloucestershire, Warwickshire and Staffordshire, settled to their new life in Southampton. After the death of her mother with whom she had lived for many years, their old friend Martha Lloyd, the elder sister of James Austen's wife Mary, also came to live with them.

We can be quite sure of the date Jane left Bath because on 30 June 1808 she wrote: 'It is two years tomorrow since we left Bath for Clifton – with what happy feelings of escape!' This remark is regularly cited as the final bit of evidence that she could not wait to get away. It is hardly surprising that, reduced to such straitened circumstances, and lodging in an insalubrious backwater, she no longer wished to be there, but that does not mean that she did not retain happy memories of her years there, years that were to prove indispensable to at least one of the three great novels she had yet to write.

I left Bath, not in a carriage, but in a train, following the route of Brunel's Great Western Railway. As I sat down the bloke behind me was loudly relating the beer-soaked events of the previous day into his mobile phone. He'd been in London for an England rugby international and had apparently done some 'seri-arse' drinking (eight pints of Guinness before the match had even kicked off, allegedly). The collateral damage was 40 fags and £120, not including his match ticket. 'I won't be telling the wife that', he confided, adding that 'he hadn't had a session like that since his wedding'. What would Jane Austen have made of a man who embarked on the holy estate of matrimony with a drinking binge? There was more than a hint of John Thorpe in his hung-over tones: 'There is not the hundredth part of the wine consumed in this kingdom, that there ought to be.'

Yes, Jane Austen even wrote about pissed men – and their wives too. She once described an incident in the Upper Rooms for the amusement of Cassandra, writing in May 1801: 'Mrs Badock & two young Women were of the same party, except when Mrs Badock thought herself obliged to leave them, to run round the room after her drunken Husband. – His avoidance, & her pursuit, with the probable intoxication of both was an amusing scene.'

I returned to Bath a couple of months later to meet three friends for lunch at the Pump Rooms. Five years before we had all lived in the same South London street and bonded through having had babies within months of each other. Now we lived on different sides of the country, and our boys had long since left their buggies and toddler groups behind in favour of football and PlayStation™. I arrived early and walked along Great

Pulteney Street in the warm spring sunshine. The paint was still peeling at 4 Sydney Place and there was no sign of life, but across the road in Sydney Gardens a group of boys, intent on Easter holiday fun, played football and cricket on the grass. 'Pitch it up this time, Oliver', urged Grandad, while Granny leaned against a nearby tree. Other children whizzed past on scooters and skateboards, and grey squirrels darted through the undergrowth, as a small army of gardeners set to work replanting the flowerbeds.

You can understand why Jane Austen loved coming here. While staying in Queen Square in 1799 she wrote that there is 'a public Breakfast in Sydney Gardens every morning, so that we shall not be wholly starved'. Later she attended a gala and fireworks in the gardens in honour of the king's birthday. In January 1801, when she and her mother were house-hunting, she wrote that 'it would be very pleasant to be near Sydney Gardens! – we might go to the Labyrinth every day.' One of the nicest things about the house they eventually found in Sydney Place must have been the view of the greenery across the road. You can't imagine it was a place to provoke depression and writer's block.

Sydney Gardens remains a delightful place to stroll, or sit a while, but it is no longer quite the pleasure garden Jane Austen knew and enjoyed. The labyrinth, grottoes and waterfalls, and the ride for those on horseback, are all long gone. The Sydney Hotel, which in Jane Austen's time was let to a Mr Holloway, who ran it 'with great spirit and liberality', now houses the Holburne Museum of Art. By the 1840s the Gardens had been sliced irrevocably down the middle by two arteries of Victorian Britain: the Kennet and Avon Canal, and the Great Western

Railway. The canal was built first, between 1796 and 1810, so it is possible that Jane Austen observed its construction while she was living in Sydney Place. Today it is a peaceful backwater, its opaque green waters slipping quietly towards Bristol under lovely old stone bridges, laced with ivy. The railway arrived three decades later, in 1841. Two hundred years after the birth of its celebrated creator, Isambard Kingdom Brunel, trains continue to thunder through the Sydney Gardens cutting, east to Paddington, west to Bristol and South Wales. Park benches offer trainspotters a front row seat at trackside level, or, if you prefer, you can look down on the show from a nearby footbridge, which is often lined with the prams and pushchairs of today's train-mad toddlers.

The Pump Room, which Catherine Morland finds 'so favourable for the... completion of female intimacy, so admirably adapted for secret discourses and unlimited confidence', seemed an appropriate place for a girls' reunion, though there is no longer any need to parade up and down, 'looking at every body and speaking to no-one', as Catherine does. As long as you don't mind queuing for a table, you can indulge in as much people-watching as you like over lunch or afternoon tea. One of my friends arrived late for our lunch, but the rest of us were unperturbed, unlike Isabella Thorpe, who admonishes Catherine for not being on time for their own meeting at the Pump Room: 'My dearest creature, what can have made you so late? I have been waiting for you at least this age.' After gossiping over hats and the latest gothic-horror novels, Isabella spots two 'odious men who have been staring at me this half hour' and drags Catherine off in hot pursuit when they leave the Pump Room.

The first Pump Room was built next to the King's Bath in 1706, and later remodelled and enlarged, first by Thomas Baldwin and then, after he went bankrupt, by John Palmer. Like the Upper and Lower Rooms, the Pump Room was a place to be and to be seen. Patrons were also able to take a glass of Bath water and peruse the arrivals book, where the names and places of abode of recent arrivals in Bath were inscribed. It is here that Catherine Morland is able to check at which house in Milsom Street the Tilneys have their lodgings. There is no such book today (how would it keep up with the coach tours and daytrippers?), but it is still possible to sample a glass of the water. At 50 pence it seems a bargain, until you realize that one sip of the nasty sulphurous stuff is enough to last a lifetime.

Though he died a pauper before their completion, it is Beau Nash, the arbiter of Bath society and fashion in the early part of the 18th century, whose statue presides over the Pump Room's lovely Georgian interior from a lofty alcove today. As waiters in waspily striped waistcoats buzzed about the room beneath another glittering chandelier, loud cheers erupted from the crowd gathered outside, drowning out the Pump Room pianist's rendering of the theme from *Doctor Zhivago*. Two street performers had stripped to leather thongs and were cavorting around the Pump Yard. Isabella Thorpe might well have quite liked it: I can certainly imagine her going outside for a good look.

On the train home I re-read the last few letters Jane Austen wrote from Bath, searching again for any indication that she was desperate to leave the city that had been her home for four years. As the sun streamed through the carriage windows onto the page, I started as the weird coincidence of that day's date flashed before my eyes. Two hundred and one years before, to the very day, Jane Austen had written to her sister at Ibthrop in Hampshire: 'Here is a day for you! Did Bath or Ibthrop ever see a finer 8th of April?... We do nothing but walk about.' Jane Austen's true feelings about Bath remain a secret, but for a few hours she and I certainly had the enjoyment of a sunny April day in one of England's most beautiful towns in common.

Chapter Three
Lyme Regis: 'A strange stranger'

The young people were all wild to see Lyme.
PERSUASION (Chapter 11)

I myself was quite wild to see Lyme Regis. I had never been there before and I knew that it was a place that Jane Austen had liked very much. Only rarely are there lengthy descriptions of real places in her novels, but in *Persuasion* she quite uncharacteristically forsakes her characters for a long paragraph in which she waxes lyrical about it. The abandoned characters are the Musgroves, Anne Elliot and Captain Wentworth who, in November 1814, embark on a one-night excursion to Lyme to visit Wentworth's naval friend, Captain Harville, and his family, who are wintering by the sea:

> They were come too late in the year for any amusement
> or variety, which Lyme, as a public place, might offer;
> the rooms were shut up, the lodgers almost all gone,
> scarcely any family but of the residents left – and, as
> there is nothing to admire in the buildings themselves,
> the remarkable situation of the town, the principal
> street almost hurrying into the water, the walk to the
> Cobb, skirting round the pleasant little bay, which in

the season is animated with bathing machines and company, the Cobb itself, its old wonders and new improvements, with the very beautiful line of cliffs stretching out to the east of the town, are what the stranger's eye will seek; and a very strange stranger's eye it must be, who does not see charms in the immediate environs of Lyme, to make him wish to know it better.

Like the party in *Persuasion*, I also came to Lyme rather late in the season, on a balmy weekend in early October. I discovered that, although the town is proud of its association with Jane Austen, it does not shout about it in the way Bath does. The exception is a notice in the town's museum, which states, a tad extravagantly, that Jane Austen's visits to Lyme in the early 1800s 'gave birth to her novel *Persuasion*'. In fact only two of the novel's 24 chapters are set in Lyme, although it's certainly true that they are pivotal and memorable ones, with Louisa Musgrove's fall from the Cobb steps a seminal Austen moment.

In January 1801, with the Austen family's decisive removal from Steventon to Bath on the horizon, Jane wrote to her sister Cassandra, telling her that she was becoming 'more and more reconciled to the idea... there is something interesting in the bustle of going away & the prospect of spending future summers by the Sea or in Wales is very delightful.'

Seaside holidays on the south coast were very much in vogue, despite the threat of Napoleonic invasion. While they were resident in Bath the Austens were among the many who made annual pilgrimages to the coast: Sidmouth in 1801, Dawlish in 1802, and then Lyme Regis for two years running, in 1803 and 1804. Of all these holidays by the sea, we have an account only of the last one, thanks to a letter that Jane wrote to Cassandra from Lyme on Friday 14 September 1804. It is a particularly significant letter, as it comes after a gap of three years in her surviving correspondence. Her previous letter is dated 26–7 May 1801 and, following the Lyme letter, there is another gaping hole until January 1805, when she picked up her pen to inform her brother Frank of their father's sudden death at Bath.

The name Lyme Regis itself has nothing to do with the Prince Regent (Jane Austen always refers to the town as Lyme, plain and simple), but dates back much earlier, to 1284, when Edward I gave the town a royal charter – 'Lyme's first great moment', as the late John Fowles calls it.[1] Fowles, who moved to Lyme in 1965 and lived there until his death in 2005, became very knowledgeable about the town's history and for many years was the curator of the town museum. He once wrote of the seaside: 'It is where one goes to spoil one's own naked body, to find sex and romance, to release, for an oblivion on all routines, fixed hours, formalities.'[2]

Why were the young people in *Persuasion* so wild to see Lyme? For those of a rambling fancy it must have been a romantic place, even a little wild; a place of pirates, and exotic comings and goings, as ship after ship docked and then set sail again. For centuries Lyme was a difficult place to reach by land. No wheeled transport could get into the town at all until the turnpike road was built in 1759. Until then everything arrived on horseback, packed into wooden boxes or large baskets. It was into these baskets – dorsers, as they were known – that Lyme fish was packed before being transported to London. 'In what state it arrived one does not like to think', John Fowles writes in his history of Lyme.[3]

By the 18th century Lyme's population had dwindled to less

than 1,000 people, while local government was in the hands of a corrupt Bristol family, the Fanes, who, according to Fowles, ran Lyme with a 'ruthless contempt'.[4] They corrupted the Lyme customs service and turned its officers into a local mafia. The Fanes were still in power at the time of Jane Austen's two visits, holding on until the Reform Act of 1832, when Lyme borough was reduced to a single MP. Two things saved Lyme from terminal decline at that time: the aforementioned turnpike road and a treatise, in Latin, on the virtues of sea water, published in 1750 by a Dr Richard Russel.

Russel's pronouncements, quickly translated into English, secured a wide readership among what would now be called the chattering classes. Russel hailed sea water as a cure-all for a wide variety of ailments, from gout to gonorrhoea (just the sort of illnesses, John Fowles points out, that the 'self-indulgent rich' increasingly suffered from).[5] This wasn't the first time that such claims had been made, but Russel's book happened to coincide with the first stirrings of the Romantic movement, with its reverence for the picturesque and the wild beauties of nature. Suddenly those who would never previously have considered a sojourn on the south coast (all those pirates, and the French just over the horizon!), started to find the prospect of a holiday beside the sea really quite enticing.

The early years of the tourist trade in Lyme received a considerable boost from the presence of a retired radical philanthropist (now there's a job description to aspire to) named Thomas Hollis, who lived nearby. In 1771, just as the Austens were moving into the rectory at Steventon, he bought land along the shoreline and created the town's first public promenade, now the eastern end of Marine Parade, but known in those days as The

Walk. Then, in 1772, the nascent seaside resort received its first celebrity endorsement when the Earl of Chatham brought his ailing son to Lyme for the sea air. The air proved highly efficacious, as that sickly boy, William Pitt the Younger, grew up to become Prime Minister.

In a few short years Lyme was transformed into a busy resort with a reputation for being cheaper and less formal than nearby Weymouth, which, despite being frequented by George III, is jokingly described by Jane in her letter from Lyme as 'altogether a shocking place... without recommendation of any kind'. Lyme acquired hotels, boarding houses, indoor baths, bathing machines, a circulating library and smart new Regency villas on the surrounding hillsides.

In the first tourist guide to the town, published in 1817 and entitled *Pictures of Lyme Regis and Environs*, its author, one M. Phillips, dwells on the charms of Lyme's 'amphitheatrical bay' and its favourable climate:

> In the spring and autumn, when the frequent variations
> of the atmosphere operate so unfavourably at most
> other fashionable resorts for sea bathing, here the fine
> hills, east, west and north, shelter the Town, which, to
> use a homely, though a true expression, is a greatcoat
> warmer than the generality of Watering-places.

Visitors to Lyme then, as now were also assured of a good fish supper: 'The excellence of Provisions in this part of England is not exceeded, and at more moderate prices than elsewhere. – Fish is abundant, and the supply regular; especially Turbot, Brill, Soles &c. The Prawns here are remarkably fine; Lobsters are abundant.'

Phillips extols the cultural assets of the town as well as its natural ones. There were three Sunday schools, 'happily calculated to instruct the ignorant, and improve the morals of the lower class of people.' The Assembly Rooms were elegant and spacious... 'over the card room, is an excellent Billiard-Room and table: – The subscriptions to these rooms are extremely moderate. The Assemblies are held on Tuesdays and Thursdays: tea and coffee to Subscribers are charged only one shilling each person. – Sedan Chairs are kept for the accommodation of the Company. – London and provincial papers are regularly taken in. – The sociability of a most respectable, liberal, and polite party of resident Inhabitants, as well as Visitants, rend it equal to other similar establishments.'

Phillips concludes: 'It is the remark of strangers who visit Lyme, that the regularity of good hours kept by the company, both at the public rooms, as well as in the private parties, contribute much to their good health; and as it is truly said, in the guide to Watering-places, that "Lodgings and Boarding at Lyme, are not merely reasonable, but cheap".'[6]

The prospect of a genteel and salutary holiday, at relatively low cost, enticed the Austens to Lyme from their home in Bath for two years in succession. By the time they made their first visit Lyme was firmly established as an excellent place in which to recuperate from the Bath summer season, all those parties and late nights having taken their toll. Consequently, high season in Lyme was considerably later than it is today: September to November. Accordingly, in 1803 the Austens arrived in November, just like the young people in *Persuasion*. As none of Jane's correspondence survives from this year, it is possible to be precise about the timing of their visit only because of a letter that Jane wrote from Southampton to Cassandra at Godmersham five years later, in October 1808. In it she describes a fire that broke out at Webbe's the pastry cook's in Southampton, which burned for some time 'with great fury', and adds: 'The flames were considerable, they seemed about as near to us as those at Lyme, & to reach higher.' There was indeed a serious fire at Lyme Regis on 5 November 1803, when part of the town round Mill Lane burned down. We do not know where the Austens lodged during this visit. In *Jane Austen and Lyme Regis*, Maggie Lane suggests that their proximity to the fire means that it was probably in the lower part of the town.[7]

In 1804 the Austen party, which that year comprised Mr and Mrs Austen, Jane, her brother Henry and his wife Eliza, was installed in Lyme by late summer. Jane wrote to Cassandra on 14 September: 'Hitherto the weather has been just what we could wish – the continuance of the dry season is very necessary to our comfort.' Initially the Austens are thought to have stayed in Pyne House at 10–11 Broad Street, a building that still stands today. It was probably vacated by its owners to provide private lodgings for the Austens. Today the low-ceilinged building has a rather unloved air. Its windows are dark and uncurtained, and serve only as advertising space for local tradesmen: 'Builder: Restoration and Repairs'; 'Fibre Glass Roofing Systems'; 'Architectural Consultants'. However, a little rectangular plaque above the front door commemorates its illustrious former tenant.

At some point Henry and Eliza left Lyme to travel with Cassandra via Weymouth to visit friends in Hampshire. Jane and her parents then left Pyne House, and transferred to cheaper lodgings elsewhere in the town. We do not know their location, but, wherever it was, Jane was not impressed: '... nothing certainly can exceed the inconvenience of its Offices, except the general Dirtiness of the House and furniture, & all it's Inhabitants'.

When I arrived in Lyme I, like the visitors in *Persuasion*, walked directly down to the sea, and 'lingering only, as all must linger and gaze on a first return to the sea, proceeded towards the Cobb'. The Cobb is Lyme's most renowned feature, famous not only from the incident in which Louisa Musgrove falls and sustains a 'severe contusion' to her head, but also as the setting for the most memorable scene in John Fowles' novel *The French Lieutenant's Woman* and Karel Reisz's film version of 1981, starring Meryl Streep and Jeremy Irons.

Though no one seems quite sure where the word 'Cobb' comes from, the distinctive curving harbour has existed in some form since the 13th century. There are no natural harbours in the broad sweep of Lyme Bay, so as soon as Lyme started to become a trading port of some importance it became necessary to create one. The original Cobb, which, according to John Fowles, was regarded as 'one of the architectural wonders of England'[8], was made of huge rounded boulders piled within walls made of oak pillars. For centuries it was actually detached from the land at high tide and not only provided a safe harbour, but also helped to protect the crumbling shore from the fury of the sea. About 50 years before Jane Austen's first visit to the town, the Cobb was joined to the land; it was rebuilt in local Portland stone in the early 19th century.

Though the harbour created by the original Cobb was not large, it was sizeable enough to make Lyme Regis the second most important port in Dorset in the 14th century. Ships arrived from across the known world: first from the Mediterranean, and later from Africa, the West Indies and North America. Lyme was the main export point for goods from a large part of southwestern England – Dorset, Somerset and Devon. John Fowles says that even the merchants of Bristol sometimes preferred to ship through Lyme, rather than risk the 'corsair-ridden Bristol Channel'.[9] The port began to decline in importance from the 18th century, mainly due to the rise of the textile industries in the North of England, but cargo ships were still steaming into Lyme as late as the 20th century.

Maintaining the Cobb has always been a major expense for the people of Lyme. When I got there the end of the upper wall of the Cobb, which curves out to sea, was closed for repairs and inaccessible behind large wire barriers, so I was immediately thwarted in my sad ambition to emulate Meryl Streep as she stands facing the sea, her all-enveloping cloak billowing in the gale. Mind you, the backdrop of large parked diggers, on hire from Axminster Excavators, would have done nothing for the atmosphere of tragic romance.

I consoled myself with the thought that the weekenders in *Persuasion* did not make it to the end of the Cobb either: 'There was too much wind to make the high part of the new Cobb pleasant for the ladies, and they agreed to get down the steps to the lower, and all were contented to pass quietly and carefully down the steep flight, excepting Louisa; she must be jumped down them by Captain Wentworth.' We know the rest – Louisa insists on being jumped down the steps a second time, misses the safe arms of the Captain, falls to the ground and is 'taken up, lifeless!'

Maggie Lane, a distinguished expert on Jane Austen, has some fun speculating from exactly which steps Louisa Musgrove comes to grief. There are three sets: the first she reckons too new and too close to the town, the second too close to the end of the Cobb, as we know that the 'young people' didn't make it to the end. That leaves the third set, the perilous Granny's Teeth.[10]

Granny's Teeth can only loosely be described as steps. They are actually roughly hewn blocks of stone set at descending levels into the side of the upper Cobb. They are not easy to negotiate in 21st-century garb, let alone in a full-length skirt, even supposing one had a gallant gentleman to hand one down. With no uniformed naval heroes in sight, Granny's Teeth presented me with a stiff challenge: my knees start to tremble on even the lowest of stepladders. Thanks to my vertigo, I failed miserably in my Austen quest at this point. I just couldn't pluck up the courage to descend Granny's Teeth and had to grit my own teeth to make it up them.

I like to think that Granny's Teeth presented no such problems for Jane Austen herself and that her description of her characters' descent of them was written from personal experience. We know from her Lyme letter that she went for a walk on the Cobb in the company of a Miss Armstrong, whose acquaintance she had recently made, perhaps at the Assembly Rooms.

When she called for Miss Armstrong on the morning of 14 September 1804, Jane passed the judgement, later related to Cassandra, that, 'Like other young Ladies, she is considerably genteeler than her Parents: Mrs Armstrong sat darning a pr of Stockings the whole of my visit.' After this unpromising start, however, Jane seems to have enjoyed her walk with her friend. Despite her companion's lack of 'Wit or Genius', she had certain agreeable qualities, namely 'Sense and some degree of taste, and her manners are very engaging', although she apparently displayed a tendency to 'like people too easily'. That is not a fault that one could find with Jane herself. The important thing is that we know she was here. Nigel Nicolson goes as far as to say that the significance of the Cobb is that it is 'the single piece of masonry in Jane Austen's fiction which can be identified for certain'.[11] Actually there are a few bits of masonry in Bath that could lay claim to easy identification too, but the Cobb certainly allows you to walk indisputably in Jane Austen's footsteps, as well as in those of her characters.

Two hundred years later Granny's Teeth are still a subject of great curiosity for visitors to the Cobb. Most express themselves 'not surprised' that Louisa Musgrove fell as she did. To my shame, I observed that few people were as easily deterred from the challenge of climbing down them as I had been. People scrambled down in droves, despite all sorts of encumbrances: babes in arms, dogs and even supermarket shopping. A line of herring gulls, perched on the top of the nearby Marine Aquarium, took no interest in the daredevils below, but barked to each other occasionally as they concentrated on patrolling the movements of fishing boats in the harbour instead.

Lyme's Marine Aquarium is home to lobsters, dogfish, some large crabs and a rippling conger eel, which, when I visited, had poked its head into the cleft of a rock at the bottom of its tank, and was refusing to come out and play. At least it is still rippling, which is more than can be said for the World Record Conger Eel, the subject of a cutting from the Angler's Mail displayed nearby. Caught off Brixham by Vic Evans in 1995, it was 8 foot long, and weighed 133 pounds and 4 ounces. Further on there is a picture of the enormous lobster found in the conning tower of a wrecked German U-boat somewhere in Lyme Bay by a builder from North London, Norman Whitehead, aged 54. 'It was mortal combat', Mr Whitehead is reported as saying. 'I had to get my hands over his back and avoid his claws, which are bigger than my builder's hands.'

The Aquarium also contains some absorbing displays about the history of seafaring in Lyme, with potted biographies of some of its most notorious smugglers, including one Jack Rattenbury, the 'Rob Roy of the West'. Rattenbury was undoubtedly active at the time of Jane Austen's visits. He married a Lyme girl in 1800 and, as our distinguished holiday-maker slept, much furtive shoreline activity must have taken place. It all goes to show that, despite its new-found veneer of gentility, Lyme was still a wild and lawless place. I like to think that this was an aspect of the town that Jane found rather exciting.

Also on view in the Aquarium are some photographs taken during the filming of the television production of *Persuasion*, shown on BBC2 in 1995. The part of Louisa Musgrove was played by Emma Roberts who, we are told, 'did all her own stunt work'. The scene in which she falls from the upper Cobb 'took hours to set up and rehearse', and indeed there is a shot of her practising her landing with the aid of a large crash-mat.

I spent a contented couple of hours ambling up and down the upper and lower Cobb, and sitting on a bollard by the harbour in the early autumn sunshine. Close by, on the wall of the Marine Aquarium, is a large sign: 'The Gods Do Not Subtract

From the Allotted Span of Mens [*sic*] Lives The Hours Spent Fishing.'

There is also a memorial to the eventful life of Admiral Sir George Somers (1554–1610), an Elizabethan seafarer, politician and military leader. Not content with fending off the Spanish Armada off the coast of Dorset, he zipped over to Venezuela to attack Caracas, popped back to give a helping hand in beating the invaders off Ireland, and then spent a few quiet years at home serving as Mayor of Lyme Regis and as its member of Parliament. Then, on a business trip to Virginia – he had been one of the founders of the London Virginia Company – he was shipwrecked by a hurricane off the coast of Bermuda, but managed to turn his misfortune to his advantage by founding England's first crown colony on the island.

There is a Bermuda connection with Jane Austen. Charles, her youngest brother, first met his future wife Fanny, then the 16-year-old daughter of the island's Attorney General, while he was stationed there with the Royal Navy. They were married in Bermuda in May 1807 and the two eldest of their four daughters, Cassandra Esten and Harriet Jane, were born on the island. Fanny was to die in 1814, giving birth to their fourth daughter, and Charles subsequently married her sister Harriet, with whom he had four more children. After a period spent in the coastguard service in Cornwall, during which he was forced to give up sailing for eight years following a fall from a mast, Charles went to sea again and died of cholera in 1852 while on active service in Burmese waters.

Admiral Somers also died abroad, in Bermuda in 1610, and, though his heart was buried on the island, his body was pickled in a barrel and returned to Lyme Regis, arriving back at the

Cobb in 1616. The memorial claims that Shakespeare wrote *The Tempest* in tribute to Somers.

After Louisa Musgrove's fall, Captain Wentworth carries her in her 'lifeless' state to the Harvilles' house, to await the arrival of a surgeon. There is a wonderful comic description of the contemporary ambulance chasers who gather to watch the scene, the general excitement of which has been further enhanced by the fainting away with shock of Louisa's sister, Henrietta Musgrove (I hope I needn't remind you of Jane Austen's views on fainting):

> By this time the report of the accident had spread among the workmen and boatmen about the Cobb, and many were collected near them, to be useful if wanted, at any rate, to enjoy the sight of a dead young lady, nay, two dead young ladies, for it proved twice as fine as the first report.

As to the location of Captain Harville's winter lodgings to which Louisa's lifeless form is transported, Maggie Lane believes that 'it is self-evidently a fictional construct… It would have seemed impertinent to her to purloin any real person's home for her fiction.'[12] Naturally this has not stopped enthusiasts from speculating as to its possible whereabouts. In Jane Austen's time the Cobb was situated some distance away from the main village of Lyme, with the few cottages nearby forming a separate settlement, known as Cobb hamlet. A row of buildings, including the Royal Standard pub, dating from that time, still stands close to the Cobb today, although they are no doubt much altered in appearance.

In *Jane Austen, Her Homes and Her Friends,* Constance Hill declares with an air of certainty that Bay Cottage, the last building in the row as you walk towards the town of Lyme, was the most likely candidate for the Harvilles' lodgings. Miss Hill even lodged there herself and reported that the landlady 'looked upon the whole matter as settled beyond a doubt'.[13] The tradition has clearly endured, as the downstairs part of the building is now called Jane's Café and Takeaway (upstairs is a pizzeria). Its diner-style tables, with their red-chequered vinyl tablecloths, afford lovely views of the coastline and the Isle of Portland, but it will disappoint those in search of some confirming period feature from Jane Austen's time. In faithful 1970s style the walls are pine-clad and hot beverages are served in flecky ironstone mugs rather than china cups. The cappuccino machine was broken, but I was quite happy enjoying the view with a mug of instant.

Staring out to sea was altogether a more worrying pursuit in 1804. It was the height of the invasion scare, when people all along the south coast of England expected Napoleon's forces to appear over the horizon at any moment. The possibility of sighting the French fleet clearly did not deter the Austens from visiting Lyme at this worrying time. Sarah Woodruff, John Fowles' French lieutenant's woman, hoped beyond hope, of course, that a Frenchman would materialize from across the water, although, as Charles Smithson soon finds out to his cost, 'her sadness' has become 'her happiness'.[14]

Beyond Jane's Café is the beach where the bathing machines were to be found in Jane Austen's time. We know for a fact that Jane enjoyed sea-bathing. In her letter of 14 September 1804 she wrote: ' The Bathing was so delightful this morning & Molly [her maid] so pressing with me to enjoy myself that I believe I staid in rather too long, as since the middle of the day I have felt unreasonably tired.' Perhaps her fatigue also had something to do with her enthusiasm for dancing the previous evening, which is reported earlier in her letter.

Sea-bathers of the time did not just splash their way into the waves in full view of the world, as they do today. First they entered a bathing machine on wheels and changed – into a shift, if you were a woman. The machine was then hauled into the water by a horse, or even by a strong man. Once they were a little way out to sea, a couple of female attendants would help the bather down into the water, where they were held under from the shoulders downwards. Dr Russel and other prominent advocates of sea-bathing were very specific about the whole process, dictating exactly how long one should remain in the water: 'The unskilful may make very bad use', he cautioned.[15]

Sea-bathing was considered particularly beneficial in cold weather and at an early hour of the morning, when the pores were supposed to be closed. In *Jane Austen and Lyme Regis* Maggie Lane quotes a Dr Crane of Weymouth: 'To Bathe late in the Day (more especially in hot Weather) will occasion great depression of Spirits.'[16] Consequently, the beach season in the seaside resorts of the time did not necessarily coincide with the busy July and August peaks of the present day. Most of us are clearly less tolerant of cold water than our forebears were and much less inclined to believe in its health-giving properties.

Among its 18th-century advocates was Jane Austen's glamorous cousin Eliza de Feuillide. Eliza spent January and February 1791 at Margate in Kent with her ailing son Hastings, on the advice of her doctor, who maintained that 'one month's bathing at this time of year was more efficacious than Six at any other'. So it seems to have proved: 'The Sea has strengthened him wonderfully & I think has likewise been of great service to myself, I still continue bathing notwithstanding the severity of the Weather and Frost and Snow, which I think somewhat courageous.'[17] I break out in goose pimples just thinking about it.

Although the General Medical Council today might have something to say about a doctor who recommended sea-bathing in January, we continue, like those in Jane Austen's time, to put great store by the benefits of sea air. Captain Wentworth never really falls out of love with Anne Elliot after she has broken off their engagement, but it is at Lyme that he begins again to 'understand himself', cast pride aside and appreciate his former betrothed once more: 'She was looking remarkably well; her very regular, very pretty features, having the bloom and freshness of youth restored by the fine wind which had been blowing on her complexion and by the animation of eye which it had also produced.' Because her improved appearance does not go unnoticed by Captain Wentworth, and indeed produces a love rival in the shape of Anne's cousin, Mr Elliot, the sea air at Lyme takes at least some of the credit for her rekindled romance with Frederick Wentworth.

Did the benefits of the sea air elsewhere on the south coast lead to romance for Jane herself? According to 'family legend' (not always the most reliable source), it was during one of her seaside holidays in Devon – perhaps at Sidmouth or Dawlish – that Jane met a man whom she felt that she could love. The story came from Cassandra, years after Jane's death, and was recorded by her niece Caroline Austen in a letter to her brother James Edward Austen-Leigh in 1869: 'In Devonshire an acquaintance was made with some very charming man – I never

heard Aunt Cass speak of anyone with such admiration – she
had no doubt that a mutual attachment was in progress between
him and her sister. They parted – but he made it plain that he
should seek them out again – & shortly afterwards, he died!'[18]
There is nothing else in writing, and the date and location are
impossible to pin down. As Claire Tomalin puts it: 'When
Caroline set down her account, forty years after she was told it,
it had become as mistily romantic as the wilder shores of Devon
itself when the weather is uncertain.'[19] Yet the perennial curiosity about Jane's own affairs of the heart means that this strange
stranger will never be able to vanish into the Channel mists.

After my coffee break at Jane's Café I had planned to visit the
cliffside gardens that commemorate Jane's Austen's association
with Lyme Regis and were opened in April 1975 in celebration
of the bicentenary of her birth. At the opening ceremony a short
play, *Miss Austen at Lyme*, written by the town's mayor, Henry
Chessell, was performed. Now, however, like the end of the
Cobb, the gardens were fenced off from public access. In fact,
the whole seafront from the Cobb to the town was being dug up
as part of West Dorset District Council's 'environmental
improvements' to 'secure the future of Lyme Regis', which
includes the building of a new seawall and two jetties. A solemn
leaflet from the tourist office, produced to explain to visitors
why their holiday destination resembles a building site, asserts
that: 'Lyme Regis is one of the most unstable and actively erod-
ing stretches of coastline in the country.' There is even a geological diagram, in case you need further convincing about the
'unstable, slippery clays' that are responsible for Lyme Regis's

inexorable slide seawards. There is good news for future holiday-makers, however: the depleted beach is soon to be replenished with 71,000 tonnes of beach shingle and 41,000 tonnes of beach sand. Meanwhile, gigantic concrete blocks sit on the shoreline, with the tide foaming in around them, as they await their ulti-mately doomed role in stemming the relentless erosion of this part of the south coast.

Lyme Regis's geological precariousness afforded the holiday-makers of Jane Austen's time another exciting attraction. The late 18th century gave birth to the science of palaeontology, as Lyme's fossil-filled and crumbling Jurassic rocks ensured a constant supply of new specimens just waiting to be unearthed. Consequently, Lyme became a mecca for fossil hunters, both professional and amateur. Many were women, among them the Philpot sisters, who came to Lyme just after the Austens in 1805 and took up residence in what is now the Mariners' Hotel in Silver Street. Their collection of fossils became famous across Europe and now forms part of Oxford University's substantial collection. The Philpots took on a protégée, a local girl named Mary Anning. She became one of the most famous fossil hunters of her time, with, as John Fowles puts it, 'a nose for valuable specimens that amounted to genius'[20]. Speculation sur-rounds the 'Anning' referred to in Jane's letter from Lyme. He is thought by some to be Richard Anning, Mary's father, though the name was not uncommon in the district then. Whoever he was, Jane remarked that he valued a lid that they had broken at Pyne House at five shillings, but this seemed to the Austens to be 'beyond the value of all the Furniture in the room'.

A few months after my visit to Lyme there was a dramatic reminder of just what a Sisyphean task West Dorset Council has taken on in trying to shore up this crumbling coast. In January 2006 a 500-foot stretch of it collapsed into the sea near Charmouth, in the biggest local landslip for 30 years. In the *Daily Mail*'s report of the incident, on 16 January, under the headline 'Cliff Collapse Terror', Graham Turner, the manager of Lyme Regis's coastguard station, is quoted as saying: 'The cliff face didn't break off with big rocks tumbling down, it simply dropped straight off. The debris wasn't solid, it had a mud-and-sand consistency – like sludge – and it flowed down just like lava.'[21] Two young boys who had been out fossil hunting had to be pulled to safety by the coastguard after sinking up to their chests in the quagmire.

Jane Austen herself was fond of the walks towards Charmouth. In her letter from Lyme she reported that the family servants, Jenny and James, are 'walked to Charmouth this afternoon'. How risky such excursions might have proved, years before coastguards and mobile phones. However, the most recent dramatic cliff fall has only served to increase the fervour of the fossil hunters. A couple of weeks later *The Guardian* reported that they were rushing to explore 'previously invisible sections of this famously fossiliferous landscape' exposed by the landslip.[22] Perhaps a new ichthyosaurus or plesiosaurus awaits the current generation of Mary Annings as they scrabble around on the cliffs of Lyme.

Thwarted in my attempt to visit the cliffside gardens, I continued along Marine Parade. Further towards the town nestle two pretty thatched cottages, painted marshmallow pink. Over the years many a devotee of Jane Austen must have been whipped into excitement by their name plaques: 'Harville Cottage' and 'Benwick Cottage'. Could these be the houses that Jane Austen had in mind when she described Captain Harville's lodgings? They certainly look more the period part than Jane's Café does. However, despite everything these chocolate-box seducers try to suggest to the contrary, they are actually stinking great red herrings, for they were not built until about 1830. It's fun to flirt with their period charm for a while, however, and you can even move in and conduct a longer affair, as Harville and Benwick Cottages are now let out to holidaymakers.

Sadly, there are no buildings to get excited about, even erroneously, on the site of Lyme's former Assembly Rooms. The Rooms, modelled on those at Bath and completed in 1775, once stood on the Bell Cliff, but were demolished in the early 20th century to make way for a car park. 'Too pleasing, alas, and too excellent a common meeting-place not to be sacrificed to that Great British God, Convenience', says John Fowles, allowing himself a little digressive rant against the town planners in *The French Lieutenant's Woman*.[23] A print of 1815 by a Mr Read, which is now on show in the town's Philpot Museum, shows a building right on the edge of the sea, with storm waves spraying up at the windows. With three glass chandeliers to light the Rooms up at night, it must have been quite a venue. Constance Hill was among the last visitors before the Rooms were pulled down: 'We visited… by daylight, and felt almost as if it were afloat, for nothing but blue sea and sky was to be seen from its many windows.'[24]

In her Lyme letter Jane writes of the Austens' attendance at a Thursday ball at the 'Rooms', for which they arrived 'a little after eight': 'My father staid very contentedly till half-past nine and then walked home with James & a Lanthorn, tho' I beleive [*sic*] the Lanthorn was not lit as the Moon was up… My Mother & I staid about an hour later.' Jane seems to have had a very satisfactory time, dancing twice with a Mr Crawford. She takes an evident pleasure in describing to Cassandra the assortment of people she might have danced with if she had stayed, including 'a new, odd looking Man who had been eyeing me for some time… I think he must be Irish by his ease.'

I stood on the spot and tried vainly to imagine the scene that moonlit night in 1804, without getting run over for my pains. A coach from Holywell in Flintshire pulled up on the site, belching exhaust fumes, and disgorged a party of pensioners, intent on ice cream and sea air. Behind me, to the delight of the crowds of weekending families, a large pantomime triceratops lumbered past. Unlike the Lyme encountered by the visitors in *Persuasion*, the town was full of 'amusement, variety and people'. Lyme was holding its annual ArtsFest and was thronged with visitors, who had come to see exhibitions by some of its many local artists, along with sideshows featuring Tanzanian acrobats, *a cappella* quartets, fire-eaters and people willing to dress up in dinosaur costumes.

Writers and artists have often visited Lyme Regis. When Alfred, Lord Tennyson came in 1867 his friends were apparently keen to show him the place where the Duke of Monmouth landed in 1685, to launch his ill-fated attempt on the crown of his uncle, James II, starting a disastrous campaign that ended at the Battle of Sedgemoor and precipitated the infamous trials presided over by Judge Jeffries. 'Don't talk to me of the Duke of Monmouth', Tennyson is reported to have said. 'Show me the exact spot where Louisa Musgrove fell.'[25] James McNeill Whistler came in September 1895, stayed at the Red Lion Hotel and chose a local girl, Rose Rendell, to model for his luminous painting *Little Rose of Lyme*.

In April 1904, a century after Jane Austen, Beatrix Potter came to Lyme. Two years into a stellar career that had begun with the publication of *The Tale of Peter Rabbit* in 1902, she went on to publish an average of two books a year for the next ten years. It is thought that she began *The Tale of Little Pig Robinson* while she was on holiday in Lyme, although it was not published until much later, in 1930. Little Pig Robinson grows up on a Devon farm called Piggery Porcombe. One day he is kidnapped on a shopping trip to the port of Stymouth and carried off to sea in a schooner, to be fattened for the captain's table. He escapes and makes a new life in the land where the Bong tree grows, thus neatly explaining why Edward Lear's owl and pussy-cat encountered a piggy-wig with the ring at the end of his nose when they arrived there on their wedding journey.

I still have a little blue bookcase containing a complete set of Beatrix Potter's Tales. *Little Pig Robinson* – no. 19 – was the longest story of them all, too long in fact to be read to me without a considerable delay till bedtime. Luckily for my parents, I preferred the shorter but much more gruesome *Tale of Samuel Whiskers*, in which Tom Kitten is trussed up in a roly-poly pudding by two horrible rats with yellow teeth. Stymouth in *Little Pig Robinson* could certainly be Lyme: it is described as a 'pretty little town… which seems to be sliding downhill in a basin of hills, all slipping seaward into Stymouth harbour, which is surrounded by quays and the outer breakwater'.[26]

While I was in Lyme Regis, however, I re-read, not Beatrix
Potter, but *Sanditon*, a fragment of an unfinished novel by Jane
Austen that, aside from a few verses, has the doleful distinction
of being the last piece of literature she wrote. She started it in
January 1817 and worked on it until 18 March, when, presumably, she found herself too ill to continue: she died exactly four
months later, on 18 July. *Sanditon* is particularly relevant to
Lyme because, besides those two chapters in *Persuasion* in which
Jane writes at length about the seaside, it is the only one of her
novels to describe a resort town. The town of the title is a 'young
and rising bathing-place' on the Sussex coast. The principal
investors in its development, among them a Mr Parker, hope
that, in time, it will become as fashionable as more established
seaside places, such as Brighton, Worthing or Eastbourne. It is,
Mr Parker believes, 'the most favoured by nature and promising
to be the most chosen by man':

> He held it indeed as certain, that no person could be
> really well, no person could be really in a state of secure
> and permanent health without spending at least six
> weeks by the sea every year... Nobody could catch cold
> by the sea, nobody wanted appetite by the sea, nobody
> wanted spirits, nobody wanted strength.

The 50-page fragment that is all that remains of *Sanditon* contains, among much else, a hilarious satire on contemporary
attitudes to medicine and health. Mr Parker's two sisters and his
brother arrive in Sanditon for a visit, and are ruthlessly lampooned for their hypochondria. Jane Austen's humour on the
subject is particularly remarkable considering that she herself
had already been ill for months. What is not pilloried, however,

is the sheer pleasure of being by the sea, so obviously enjoyed by her more sensible characters, among them Charlotte Heywood, who, on her arrival in the town, stands 'at her ample Venetian window… looking over the miscellaneous foreground of unfinished buildings, waving linen, and tops of houses, to the sea, dancing and sparkling in sunshine and freshness'.

Carol Shields, the late Canadian novelist who was a great admirer of Jane Austen, wrote in her biography:

> *Sanditon*, though unfinished, shows the direction in which Jane Austen might have moved had she lived longer. In it she exploits her greatest gifts, her management of dialogue and her skill with monologue … and there is a sense that Jane Austen welcomed this new social vitality and that she may have been on the cusp of widening her novelistic scope.[27]

Late that afternoon I sat outside at a café table on the seafront at Lyme, with my copy of *Sanditon* open next to a plate of fish and chips, and soaked up the last rays of late summer sunshine. I had celebrated my 40th birthday the previous week and felt very humble when I reflected on what wonderful things Jane Austen had already written by the time she was the same age, and almost at the end of her life. It is true that when you read *Sanditon* you cannot resist wondering what gems might have followed if she had not died so young.

Jane Austen lived another 13 years after her visit to Lyme Regis in 1804, but memories of her pleasant stay there must always have been tinged with sadness. It proved to be the last seaside holiday spent in the company of her father, the man who had given Jane her first writing desk and unfailingly encouraged her literary endeavours. George Austen died suddenly in January 1805. His death heralded a period of upheaval for his widow and daughters, as well as a worrying time of even greater financial insecurity. Holidays by the sea became a thing of the past for Jane.

Chapter Four

Godmersham: 'The only place for happiness'

*Let me shake off vulgar cares & conform to the happy
Indifference of East Kent wealth.* – Letter to her sister
Cassandra, 25 September 1813

Godmersham Park, the magnificent home of Jane Austen's
brother Edward, lies buried in the East Kent countryside just off
the A28, halfway between Ashford and Canterbury. Traffic and
trains alike hurtle along the valley of the River Stour, oblivious
to the 18th-century gem that is concealed only yards away down
a tiny lane. This isn't surprising: Godmersham Park isn't marked
on any tourist maps, because it isn't open to the public, unless
you happen to be an optician in the raw. Its grand rooms are
now let out to the Association of British Dispensing Opticians
(ABDO), which uses the house as a training college. To my
excitement, however, I managed to obtain permission to look
around. Happily, the owner, John Sunley is very aware of
Godmersham's august associations and allows occasional organ-
ized visits by prior arrangement.

On the train from Charing Cross, as the drab sprawl of
London's suburbs gave way to the orchards and oast houses of

the Garden of England, I re-read some of the things Jane Austen wrote about Kent. For example, shortly after returning to Steventon from her first visit to Godmersham, in December 1798, she complained that: 'People get so horribly poor & economical in this part of the World that I have no patience with them. Kent is the only place for happiness. Everybody is rich there.'

Jane's brother Edward first attracted the notice of the wealthy Thomas Knight and his wife when they visited their distant cousins the Austens during their wedding journey in 1779. The Knights were so taken with 12-year-old Edward that they invited him to accompany them on the rest of their journey. When it became clear that they were not going to have children of their own the Knights decided to adopt him as their heir. The adoption was formally agreed upon in 1783. A portrait of the teenage Edward by the well-known society painter George Romney, commissioned to mark the occasion, can now be seen at Chawton Cottage. Life for Edward was transformed. Instead of going to university like his elder brother James, he began preparing for the life of a landed gentleman. He was sent abroad on the Grand Tour and travelled for the next four years, spending a year studying in Dresden. He was in Switzerland in 1786 and Rome in 1789, returning to England only in 1790, at the age of 23. At the end of the following year he married Elizabeth Bridges, the daughter of a Kentish baronet, Sir Brook Bridges of Goodnestone Park, east of Canterbury. The newlyweds spent their early married life at nearby Rowling, a small country house owned by the Bridges family. Four children – Fanny, Edward, George and Henry – were born there in quick succession.

Thomas Knight died in 1794 and in 1797 his widow decided

to remove herself from Godmersham Park to White Friars, a house in Canterbury, thereby allowing Edward to accommodate his growing family in a house of much grander proportions, although, strictly speaking, he would inherit Godmersham Park only on her death. Elizabeth was soon pregnant again: her first child to be born at Godmersham was her fourth son, William, who arrived in October 1798. He was later to become rector of Steventon and the father of the three little girls so tragically commemorated by the memorial in the church there.

Jane visited her brother during the summers of 1794 and 1796, when he and his family were still at Rowling. Several gossipy letters to Cassandra survive from the latter visit. On 1 September she wrote: 'The letter which I have this moment received from you has diverted me beyond moderation. I could die laughing at it, as they used to say at school. You are indeed the finest comic writer of the present age.' She went on to report that there was shooting at Godmersham for the men ('there are a prodigious number of birds hereabouts this year') and plenty of sewing for the women ('We are very busy making Edward's shirts and I am proud to say that I am the neatest worker'), and that liqueurs were drunk in the evening. Little Edward was 'breeched… for good & all, and… whipped, into the Bargain'. Jane had attended a ball at Goodnestone and fretted about whether to tip Richis, a servant at Rowling, half a guinea (ten shillings and sixpence) or only five shillings when she left: 'Counsel me, amiable Miss Austen', she implored. She also enjoyed herself updating Cassandra on local births, marriages and deaths, in a vein more entertaining than strictly informative: 'Mr Children's two Sons are both going to be married, John & George. – They are to have one wife between them; a Miss Holwell, who belongs to the Black Hole at Calcutta.' Miss Holwell's grandfather was a survivor of the notorious Calcutta siege and John George Children was in fact a single individual. 'Mr Richard Harvey's match', Jane added, wickedly, 'is put off until he has got a Better Christian name.'

People have peculiarly strong personal feelings about names, which can carry a whole raft of different associations for different individuals. Just occasionally we get a hint of Jane Austen's own likes and dislikes, as in Mansfield Park: 'There is nobleness in the name of Edmund. It is a name of heroism and renown – of kings, princes and knights; and seems to breathe the spirit of chivalry and warm affections.' For reasons not explained, Richard was a name she disliked. In the opening paragraph of Northanger Abbey we learn that Catherine Morland's father is a 'very respectable man, though his name was Richard'.

In her book *Jane Austen and Names* Maggie Lane reflects on Jane's preferences when naming her characters. The same names occur over and over again, even, as Lane points out, within the same novel: there are four Johns in *Sense and Sensibility*, three Toms and a Thomas in *Mansfield Park*, and, in *Persuasion*, five boys or men named Charles and four Marys. Partly this reflects the tradition of calling sons and daughters after their parents, but in general there were far fewer names in circulation than today, particularly for men, so Jane's limited range reflects the reality of 18th-century nomenclature. On the whole, Lane concludes, Jane's 'worthy characters have plain unpretending names, such as would not draw attention to themselves'. These are the Annes, Elizabeths, Catherines and Janes. Sometimes those with a certain name share characteristics ('her Henrys are rarely without charm', Lane notes), but more usually the names she uses can be bestowed just as well on a cad, such as George Wickham, as on an upright man, such as George Knightley.[1]

Completed in 1732, Godmersham Park was designed by an unknown architect (though Roger Morris, who designed Marble Hill in Twickenham, has been suggested as a possible candidate). The sweeping carriage drive by which one approached the house from the north, as shown in a print of 1790, no longer exists. Instead, having turned off the A28, you sneak up on it from the south, passing first the village church, then a 15th-century barn now converted into a house and, finally, the old vicarage, now hidden behind a hedge of laurel and yew. At the gates of the house the road turns away and crosses an ancient stone bridge over the River Stour before rejoining the A28. It is a hidden gem of a backwater, nestling among the wooded pillows of the North Downs as they march to meet the sea at the White Cliffs of Folkestone and Dover, a few miles away.

Through the gates a walled drive, lined with espaliers of venerable old plum trees, led to the estate office, where I found Greg Ellis, who has been estate manager at Godmersham for the past 18 years, a black Labrador at his feet. Greg kindly offered to help me get my bearings by driving me around the park in his low-slung Subaru estate. Rather sweetly, he professed himself a philistine who had never read any of Jane Austen's novels, but I discovered that he knew plenty about the Godmersham of her day and was able to quote from her letters.

First we bounced across a thistly field and up the wooded mound known as Temple Hill, after the classical summerhouse that nestles among the trees that crown the hilltop. It was built in Doric style by Thomas Knight in about 1770 and is said to have been a favourite haunt of Jane's. Its classical white outline adds just the right amount of interest to the greenness of the vista. Below its portico is a series of motifs that survive in as sharp relief as the day they were cast. In the middle of the series is a mysterious pattern of initial letters. Various attempts have been made to decipher them, though the only combination I could easily recognize was 'EA', standing for Edward Austen.

The motifs are made from Coade stone, an artificial stone material used for many types of monuments and other objects during the 18th and early 19th centuries. The brains behind the commercial production of Coade stone belonged to one Eleanor Coade, a native of Lyme Regis. Known, although she never married, as Mrs Coade, she became that rare thing, a female captain of industry in the 18th century. When George III celebrated the 50th year of his reign in 1809, several towns ordered copies of his statue in Coade stone, after Weymouth had commissioned the original to commemorate the royal patronage which led to the town's rise to fame. (George III had visited the town 14 times between 1789 and 1805.) The surviving letter that Jane wrote to Cassandra at Weymouth while holidaying in Lyme Regis refers to her sister's disappointment at having missed seeing the king embarking on the royal yacht. When completed, the life-sized statue of the King, flanked by a lion and a unicorn couchant, was erected on the esplanade. He still welcomes holidaymakers to Weymouth from his plinth today.

The interior walls of the temple had recently been painted with garish murals on a Jane Austen theme, which were not to my taste. It is the views that are the chief glory of Temple Hill. From this vantage point the whole Godmersham estate is visible, in a glorious panorama virtually unchanged in more than 200 years. Greg wanted to know whether I was getting any 'vibes'. I certainly was.

Nowadays sheep rather then deer predominate in the park, although fallow deer still make a nuisance of themselves by nibbling the corn and tearing at young trees, which have to be protected with strong wooden fences. We drove past the house and up a neighbouring hill as far as Deer Lodge, the former parkkeeper's cottage, now used as the headquarters for a stud farm. Along the top of this ridge runs the North Downs Way. On a visit to Godmersham in June 1808 with Mrs James Austen, Jane initiated her sister-in-law into the 'mysteries of Inman-ism'. Mrs Inman was the blind widow of a former clergyman at Godmersham who lived in the park-keeper's cottage. She used to walk around the grounds with a gold-headed walking stick, leaning on the arm of her servant. For the children at Godmersham it was a treat to be allowed to take some fruit up to Mrs Inman after finishing dessert.

Back past the house we veered off the track again towards a new plantation, alive with dozens of twittering young pheasants being raised for the frequent shoots that provide income for the estate. Hidden in a nearby clearing is the icehouse, a remarkable egg-shaped brick building set partly underground. I struggled out of the car, stinging my bare ankle on a nettle, and peered over a railing into the pitch-black depths of the egg. It faces north and is surrounded by oak trees, planted to provide shade. Greg told me that experiments had shown that ice could be kept here for up to 13 months. The ice was probably formed in the man-made depression in front of the ice-house and then packed inside between alternate layers of straw, to be chipped away at by a servant when required for the table. It could also have come from the nearby River Stour when it froze over in the winter. Ice was, of course, a great luxury 200 years ago. Jane conveyed what a treat it was when she wrote from Godmersham in 1808: 'I shall eat Ice & drink French wine, & be above Vulgar Economy.'

My visit to Godmersham Park coincided with the summer break for ABDO's training college, so I was able to spend some time looking around the ground floor of the house itself. Despite its handsome stone pediment and Ionic columns, the central entrance door on the north front seems impossibly narrow for such a grand house. I squeezed through and got my bag stuck in my eagerness to set eyes on the elaborate white plasterwork of the entrance hall, which remains exactly as it was when the central and earliest part of the house was built in 1732, on the site of an earlier Elizabethan residence, by Thomas May Knight, the father of Edward Austen's benefactor. I stared up at the elaborately encrusted walls, and down at the black-and-white tiles of the marble floor, in awe. Not even ABDO's display boards or the fire extinguishers that guarded each side of the door could detract from the thrill of standing in the very room where so many Austen reunions had taken place.

Here her brother and sister-in-law, and their growing band of children greeted Jane, after her long journeys from Steventon, Southampton and Chawton. There was certainly a reception committee when she arrived for her visit with Mrs James Austen in June 1808. She wrote to Cassandra, who was in Southampton: 'Our two brothers [Edward and James] were walking before the house as we approached, as natural as life. Fanny and Lizzy met us in the Hall with a great deal of pleasant joy; we went for a few minutes into the breakfast parlour, and then proceeded to our rooms.' In the course of another visit to Godmersham a few years later, in October 1813, it was Jane her self who did the meeting and greeting when her brother Charles arrived to stay with his family: 'They came last night at about 7… We met them in the Hall.' The party had had a 'very rough passage' and Cassy, Jane's four-year-old niece, was 'too tired & bewildered just at first to seem to know anybody… but before we reached the Library, she kissed me very affectionately - & has since seemed to recollect me in the same way. It was quite an evening of confusion as you may suppose – at first we were all walking about from one part of the House to the other – then came a fresh dinner in the Breakfast room for Charles and his wife.'

Although the entrance hall continues to resound with the bustle of arrivals and departures, the rest of the house has been much altered over the years. The door that faces you as you stand in the hall with your back to the entrance used to lead into a rear hall, where the house's two staircases were located. Beyond them another door led out to the terrace and gardens at the rear of the house. Constance Hill came here in the early 20th century, recording her visit in her book *Jane Austen: Her Homes and Her Friends*. In a drawing of the hall by her sister, Ellen Hill, the gardens can clearly be seen through this open door at the rear. [2] Today the staircases are gone and a sign on the door to the rear hall reads: 'Ophthalmic Lens Laboratory'. Inside I discovered no staircases, but instead rank upon rank of study tables, a lens meter standing at the ready on each one. Kodak advertising posters lined the walls and the windows were veiled with black-out blinds. It was a strange sight.

The breakfast room where Charles and his wife took their late dinner was probably the room next door, now a technology library for the college. Beyond it lie the relocated staircase and an orangery, a sympathetic 20th-century addition, now a canteen. It was empty except for a few tables and a tea urn.

To the left of the entrance hall is the former drawing room. A photocopier lurks behind the door and the walls are lined with smiling photographic portraits of past presidents of ABDO. A pretty cabinet to the left of the fireplace houses a display of old spectacles. The grey marble fireplace looked original, however: I ran my hand over its beautifully carved motif of two overflowing cornucopias and gazed out of the window.

To the right of the entrance hall is the room now used as a reception room by ABDO. I went in there to ask permission of the secretary to take photographs. While we were talking a red Parcelforce truck came up the drive and squeaked to a halt outside. In Jane Austen's time this was the dining room from which, as she described in one of her letters, she once saw Mrs Inman's chaise crossing the park while she was at dinner.

A number of other rooms are mentioned by Jane, notably the library, which was housed in one of the two elegant wings added to either side of the original building by Thomas Knight during the 1780s. The library was Jane's favourite room at Godmersham, being warm, quiet and cosy. While she was staying there during June and July 1808 there was an unexpected spell of 'cold, disagreeable weather'. Jane continued to take evening walks in the park, wrapped up in her 'kerseymere Spencer', a short double-breasted overcoat in fine wool. 'I dare say you have Fires every day', she wrote to Cassandra. Indoors, this being Godmersham, no expense was spared as to fires: 'It is now half past Twelve, and having heard Lizzy read, I am now moved down into the Library for the sake of a fire... & here in warm & happy solitude proceed to acknowledge this day's Letter'. She was to be found there again in September 1813: 'We live in the Library except at Meals & have a fire every Evening'; and, later, 'I am now alone in the Library, Mistress of all I survey.' During the same visit, which lasted several months, she managed to get the room to herself again: 'At this present time I have five Tables, Eight & twenty Chairs & two fires all to myself.'

This description reminds us just how grand a house Godmersham was in its heyday. Jane was accustomed to a comfortable but frugal life with her mother and sister, so it is hardly surprising that she lapped up her brother's kind hospitality and largesse. In October 1808 she wrote to Cassandra: 'In another week I shall be at home – & then, my having been at Godmersham will seem like a Dream. In the meantime for Elegance & Ease & Luxury.' Occasionally, however, there were inescapable reminders that she was the poor relative. A visiting hairdresser, Mr Hall, charged Jane's sister-in-law Elizabeth the extortionate sum of five shillings every time he dressed her hair, 'allowing,' Jane wrote in August 1805, 'nothing for the pleasures of his visit here, for meat, drink & Lodging', and the 'benefit of Country air'. However he charged Jane only two shillings and sixpence for cutting her hair: 'He certainly respects either our Youth or our poverty', Jane joked to Cassandra.

One of the permanent servants at Godmersham, Susanna Sackree, is mentioned several times in Jane's letters. Known as 'Caky', Sackree was nursemaid to all Edward's children and remained a fixture at Godmersham for almost 60 years until her death in 1851, aged 90. A memorial to her outside Godmersham Church is now illegible and these days she is commemorated by an illuminated scroll that hangs inside the church, the work of a modern calligrapher, Hazel Jones, from the nearby hamlet of Bilting. 'In Memory of Susanna Sackree,' it reads, 'The faithful servant and friend for nearly 60 years of Edward Knight of Godmersham Park, and the beloved nurse of all his children.' 'I told Sackree', Jane wrote to Cassandra in June 1808, 'that you desired to be remembered to her which pleased her; and she sends her duty and wishes you to know that she has been into the great world. She went on to town after taking William to Eltham, and, as well as myself, saw the ladies go to court on the 4th. She had the advantage, indeed, of me in being in the Palace.'

During her visit in 1805 Jane struck up a friendship with another member of the Godmersham staff, Fanny's governess, Miss Anne Sharp. Miss Sharp's time in Edward Austen's employ was relatively short: having arrived early in 1804, she had to resign in the spring of 1806 due to continued ill health. Jane missed her during her subsequent visits – 'three years ago we were more animated with you and Harriot and Miss Sharpe', she wrote to Cassandra in June 1808 – and the two women continued to correspond until Jane died in 1817. Jane also sent her copies of her novels when they were published: Miss Sharp's favourite was *Pride and Prejudice*. A few days after Jane's death Cassandra sent Miss Sharp a lock of Jane's hair and a bodkin that she had used for more than 20 years. Cassandra told her: 'I know how these articles, trifling as they are, will be valued by you & I am very sure that if she is now conscious of what is passing on earth it gives her pleasure they should be so disposed of.'[3]

Anne Sharp led the life of a governess and lady's companion so dreaded by Jane's poor female characters, such as Jane Fairfax in *Emma* or Elizabeth Watson in *The Watsons*. After leaving Kent she acted as companion to the crippled Miss Bailey, of Hinckley, Leicestershire, for several years, before becoming a governess again, this time to the four children of the recently widowed Lady Pilkington in Yorkshire, from 1811 onwards. Anticipating Charlotte Brontë by some years, Jane nurtured dreams of a match between Miss Sharp and the new baronet, Sir William Pilkington, and wrote in June 1814: 'I do so want him to marry her!... Oh Sir William – Sir William – how I will love you, if you will love Miss Sharp.' There was to be no romance, however. By 1823 the much-travelled Miss Sharp had crossed the Pennines and was running her own boarding school for girls in Everton Terrace in Liverpool. She remained in that city until her death in 1853.

I can't decide whether Jane, the poor relative, felt really at home at Godmersham or not, despite its being all 'Elegance & Ease & Luxury'. She remarks at one point in June 1808: 'Edward certainly excels in doing the Honours to his visitors, & providing for their amusement.' Yet it's interesting that she seems to have gravitated more naturally towards the company of Miss Sharp, rather than that of the grand but dull representatives of Kent society who came calling, and to whom the family paid an endless round of visits in return: 'I have discovered that Lady

Elizabeth for a woman of her age and situation has astonishingly little to say for herself, & that Miss Hatton has not much
more'; 'Mrs Britton called here on Saturday... She is a large,
ungenteel Woman, with self-satisfied & would-be elegant manners'; 'We have got rid of Mr R Mascall… I did not like him
either. He talks too much & is conceited – besides having a vul-
garly shaped mouth.'

The duration of Jane's visits to Godmersham was certainly a
source of frustration at times. Her letters record occasions when
she felt stranded, her travel arrangements completely out of her
hands. She couldn't go home until her father or one of her
brothers was able to take her. Either it was months before a
suitable opportunity arose, or she was snatched away from Kent
far too soon. During her visit to Rowling in September 1796,
for example, her plans were thrown into chaos when her
brother Frank, who was to take her to stay with her friends the
Pearsons in London, was recalled to his ship unexpectedly early.
Jane could not go with him to town, as there was a risk that
she would be left stranded with nowhere to stay, and: 'If the
Pearsons were not at home, I should inevitably fall a Sacrifice
to the arts of some fat Woman who would make me drunk
with Small Beer.' She had to hope instead that her father would
come to town to 'fetch home his prodigal Daughter'. In June
1808, no sooner had she arrived to stay at Godmersham than
she was summoned to Edward's study to discuss how she was to
get back to Southampton again. She was told that she had to
leave with Edward when he set off on a business trip to Alton,
but wrote: 'I should have preferred a rather longer stay here certainly, but there is not prospect of any later conveyance for me.'
There was no possibility either of calling in on cousins in Kent

and Surrey on the way, as she had hoped to do. 'Till I have a travelling purse of my own, I must submit to such things', she wrote, resignedly.

It was the same for Cassandra, though it seems that she may have been more welcome at Godmersham than Jane was. The sisters were rarely there at the same time, and Cassandra was invariably the one called upon to attend Elizabeth during her confinements and to help look after the children. Cassandra was at Godmersham when Elizabeth died in October 1808 and was prevailed upon to remain there well into the New Year.

In her *Recollections of Aunt Jane*, published in 1864, Anna Lefroy wrote:

> Aunt Jane was generally the favourite with children, but with the young people of Godmersham it was not so. They liked her indeed as a playfellow, & as a teller of stories, but they were not really fond of her. I believe their mother was not; at least she very much preferred the elder sister. A little talent went a long way with the Goodnestone Bridges of that period; and *much* must have gone a long way too far.[4]

It's difficult to know how reliable this account is. Anna was less often at Godmersham than her aunt was, and Jane does seem to have had plenty of enjoyable times in Kent, playing shuttlecock with her nephews or giggling over her latest novel with her nieces. A letter written years later by her favourite niece, Fanny, of whom she was inordinately fond, is more shocking. She remembered that Jane

was not so refined as she ought to have been from her

talent... Both the Aunts were brought up in the most complete ignorance of the World & its ways (I mean as to fashion &c) & if it had not been for Papa's marriage which brought them into Kent... they would have been, tho' not less clever and agreeable in themselves, very much below par as to good Society and its ways.[5]

As a young woman Fanny was only to ready too enjoy the way in which her Aunt Jane poked fun at 'good Society and its ways' in her novels. Unfortunately, she seems to have grown up into a rather stolid Victorian lady.

Jane mentions a number of the upstairs rooms at Godmersham Park. During her stay in June 1808 her sister-in-law Mary was given the hall chamber (presumably the one immediately above the entrance hall) and Jane had the 'Yellow Room'. There are also references to a 'White Room' and 'a little chintz room', the latter created after a redecoration programme instituted by Edward in 1813. While the house was being repainted he removed his family to Chawton away from the paint fumes, which in those days were capable of causing a mild form of lead poisoning known as 'painter's colic'. In July that year Jane wrote: 'My Brother will probably go down & sniff at it himself & receive his Rents.'

During this same period of renovation, a billiard room was created in one of the wings. It swiftly proved a great attraction on Edward's return: 'The Comfort of the Billiard Table here is very great. – It draws all the Gentlemen to it whenever they are within, especially after dinner, so that my Brother, Fanny and I have the Library to ourselves in delightful quiet', wrote Jane in October 1813. Among the devotees was Edward's brother-in-law Edward Bridges, who, it is rumoured, had proposed marriage to Jane some years before. In August 1805 she wrote: 'It is impossible to do justice to the hospitality of his attentions towards me... he made a point of ordering toasted cheese for supper entirely on my account.' Edward Bridges subsequently married the daughter of a London banker, but Jane hinted in a letter of October 1813 that it was not a success: 'We have had another of Edward Bridges' Sunday visits. – I think the pleasantest part of his married Life, must be the Dinners & Breakfasts & Luncheons & Billiards that he gets in this way at Godmersham.'

The configuration of the first-floor rooms at Godmersham has changed beyond recognition, making it virtually impossible to identify any of the rooms Jane mentions in her letters. The library too was split up into smaller rooms during the 1930s, so, sadly, the room where Jane worked on *Mansfield Park* and *Emma* in such comfort no longer exists. One of her Godmersham nieces, Marianne, described years later how her aunt

> used to bring the MS of whatever novel she was writing with her, and would shut herself up with my elder sisters in one of the bedrooms to read them aloud. I and the younger ones used to hear peals of laughter through the door, and thought it very hard that we should be shut out from what was so delightful. I also remember how Aunt Jane would sit quietly working beside the fire in the library, saying nothing for a good while, and then would suddenly burst out laughing, jump up and run

across the room to a table where pens and paper were lying, write something down, and then come back to the fire and go on quietly working as before.[6]

Jane's visits to Godmersham must have provided her with valuable insights into life in a great country residence. 'In this house,' she wrote to her brother Frank in September 1813, 'there is a constant succession of small events, somebody is always going or coming.' Frank himself arrived for a visit in July 1806, bringing with him his new bride, the erstwhile Mary Gibson of Ramsgate. Jane wrote a poem on the occasion for Fanny's amusement:

> Down the hill they're swift proceeding
> Now they skirt the park around;
> Lo! The Cattle sweetly feeding
> Scamper, startled at the sound!
>
> Run, my Brothers, to the Pier gate!
> Throw it open, very wide!
> Let it not be said that we're late
> In welcoming my Uncle's Bride!
>
> To the house the chaise advances;
> Now it stops – They're here, they're here!
> How d'ye do, my uncle Francis?
> How does do your Lady dear?

Although she was of humbler origins, Mary Austen, *née* Gibson, was to share the same fate as her sister-in-law Elizabeth. Each of them gave birth to 11 children in the space of 15 years and, in a macabre parallel, it was the 11th birth that cost each of them their lives. Mary's baby Cholmeley, born in July 1823, lived for six months, but his mother died only a week after giving birth to him. Elizabeth Austen gave birth to her 11th child, Brook John, at Godmersham on 28 September 1808, when she was 35. Cassandra was staying in Kent at the time. On 1 October Jane wrote to her sister from Southampton: 'We are extremely glad to hear of the birth of the Child, and trust everything will proceed as well as it begins.' On 10 October, shortly after eating a hearty dinner, Elizabeth was taken ill and died within hours. It was a shattering blow. Jane pictured her brother at Godmersham, 'restless in Misery going from one room to the other – & perhaps not seldom upstairs to see all that remains of his Elizabeth'.

Death either during or following childbirth was horribly common in Jane Austen's time and, even if they survived almost yearly labours with little medical assistance, constant pregnancies took their toll on women's minds and bodies. Jane Austen never had any children herself, of course, but she saw plenty of evidence of maternal suffering around her and was moved to several comments in her letters, to the effect that husbands should learn the meaning of abstinence. Only a week before Elizabeth's death, Jane had responded thus to reports that Mrs Tilson, the 31-year-old wife of Henry's banking partner, was pregnant once more, with her seventh child: 'Poor woman! how can she honestly be breeding again?'; and in February 1807 she had written from Southampton: 'That Mrs Deedes is to have another Child I suppose I may lament' (Mrs Deedes was the elder sister of Edward's deceased wife Elizabeth). With every new pregnancy in the family spinsterhood may well have seemed a more and more attractive state. She wrote of Frank's wife in September 1816: 'Mrs FA seldom either looks or appears quite well. Little Embryo is troublesome, I suppose.' A few months later in March 1817 she exhorted her niece Fanny not to rush into marriage or motherhood: 'By not beginning the business of Mothering quite so early in life, you will be young in Constitution, spirits, figure and countenance.'

It was too late to dispense such advice to another of her nieces, Anna. Having given birth to her first daughter in October 1815, some ten months after her marriage to Ben Lefroy, and to her second in September 1816, Anna was in the family way again by March 1817. Jane commented: 'Anna has not a chance of escape... Poor Animal, she will be quite worn out before she is thirty. – I am very sorry for her.' Anna was not the only one. Jane continued: 'Mrs Clement too is in that way again. I am quite tired of so many Children. – Mrs Benn has a 13th.' Jane was no Marie Stopes, but she certainly understood the benefits of birth control and wrote to Fanny in February 1817: 'I would recommend to her and Mrs D, the simple regimen of separate rooms.' 'Mrs D' was Mrs Deedes (already mentioned above), who had just given birth to her 18th child.

I stepped out of the house and went to sit on the front lawn in the sunshine to eat the lunch I had bought earlier from a sandwich bar in the Strand. I looked around and realized that I was probably sitting in the middle of the old carriage drive that once swept up to the house, but of which there is now not the slightest trace. Behind me the ground fell away sharply where a ha-ha had recently been dug to keep the sheep at bay. A solitary seagull stood nearby, its tail feathers ruffling in the strong breeze. From high above came the muffled roar of aircraft well into their ascents from Gatwick. All around me grasshoppers clicked in the long grass.

Godmersham Park is not open to visitors, but a public foot-path runs through the estate, affording an excellent view of the house to anyone prepared to walk. I set off along it. A lone sheep penned on one side of the path was conversing loudly with a friend in a nearby field as I strode up the hillside. A track lined with electric fences, disguised behind beech and hawthorn hedges, gave way to grass verges stuffed with wild flowers and a field of ripe golden wheat beyond. Peacock butterflies flickered across my path. At Deer Park Cottage a line of washing flapped in the breeze and a set of cricket stumps had been hammered deep into the mossy earth in the shade of a tree. At a stile my way was blocked by a posse of four sheep, which stared me out, only skittering away at the last moment. They trotted away only a few steps before turning back for one more look, like ovine versions of Lot's wife. I sat on top of the stile for a while and they soon wandered back. There were two newly shorn ewes, each with a lamb at her heels, still intent on suckling despite being almost fully grown. I looked down at the impossibly pastoral scene below: sheep in the foreground, patchwork of fields and gentle wooded hills in the background. As I contemplated this Arcadian scene, a completely unexpected sense of joy welled up inside me. No wonder Elizabeth Bennet begins to change her mind about Darcy when she looks down on a similarly idyllic scene at Pemberley for the first time:

> They gradually ascended for half a mile, and then found themselves at the top of a considerable eminence, where the wood ceased, and the eye was instantly caught by Pemberley House, situated on the opposite side of a val-

ley, into which the road with some abruptness wound.
It was a large, handsome stone building, standing well
on rising ground, and backed by a ride of high woody
hills... Elizabeth was delighted. She had never seen a
place for which nature had done more, or where natural
beauty had been so little counteracted by an awkward
taste... at the moment she felt, that to be mistress of
Pemberley might be something!

I walked back down the hillside with the wind at my back. The
grey roofs and tall chimneys of Godmersham Park came back
into view. I thought of all that had gone on within its walls – the
dinners, the parties, the births, the deaths – and all because one
day, in a rectory in Hampshire, the visiting Knights saw potential in a clergyman's young son.

   Edward Austen did not take the name of Knight until after
Mrs Knight's death in 1812. His daughter Fanny was not
pleased with the change: 'We are all therefore Knights instead of
dear old Austens! How I hate it!!!!!'[7] Jane herself wrote more
neutrally of the alteration in November 1812: 'We have reason
to suppose the change of name has taken place, as we have to
forward a Letter to Edward Knight Esq from the Lawyer who
has the management of the business. I must learn to make a better K.' Jane had more reason to lament the death of Mrs Knight,
of whom she had been very fond. She had often called on her at
her house, the White Friars in Canterbury, while she was at
Godmersham and had even stayed the night on occasions. 'It
was a very agreeable visit,' she wrote in June 1808. 'There was
everything to make it so – kindness, conversation, variety, without care or cost.' It seems that Mrs Knight may also have been
Jane's one and only patron: during the same visit Jane mentions

receiving a letter from her 'containing the usual Fee' and adds: 'Her very agreeable present will make my circumstances quite easy.'

Round the south side of the house sturdy wooden fencing gives way to a high brick wall that surrounds the inner park and gardens. The wall had to be substantially rebuilt in places after the great storm of 1987, which also decimated the Wilderness, and its avenue of lime and yew trees known in Jane Austen's time as Bentigh. In June 1808 Jane wrote: 'Yesterday passed quite a la Godmersham: the gentlemen rode about Edward's farm, and returned in time to saunter along Bentigh with us.' Returning to Godmersham in September 1813, after an absence of four years, she wrote: 'How Bentigh is grown!' After the destruction of so many trees in 1987 the avenue was replanted on a slightly different axis, with the help of a grant from English Heritage, and now a new leafy thoroughfare slopes away towards the house, behind an elegant pair of black gates.

I walked down to Godmersham's pretty flint church, dedicated to St Lawrence the Martyr, and dating in part from Saxon and Norman times. The churchyard slopes down to the River Stour and its lowest headstones look across its waters as if longing to get to the other side. Inside the church there are memorials to Edward Austen's benefactor Thomas Knight and his wife Catherine, and to Edward himself: 'Living peaceably in his habitation, he was honoured in his generation/A merciful man, whose righteousness shall not be forgotten.' A door next to the pulpit leads to a beautiful 12th-century Norman chapel, below the bell tower. Bell-ringing sequences were Blu-Tacked to the walls, alongside a chart for the recently completed 2006 football World Cup.

The other buildings in Godmersham village line the road that leads to the great house. Jane would recognize most of them still, including the converted barn and the old vicarage (mentioned above). The only thing that she might find confusing is that the vicar now lives in the old forge: the original vicarage is no longer in church hands (hence the 'old' in front of its name). The blue door in the wall opposite leads straight into the grounds of Godmersham Park and is known as 'Mr Collins's door'.

In *Pride and Prejudice* the fictional parish of Hunsford in Kent is home to the imperious Lady Catherine de Bourgh and to Mr Collins, a parson and cousin of the Bennet sisters. After Elizabeth Bennet's friend and neighbour, Charlotte Lucas, contains her aspirations and marries the preposterous Collins ('I am convinced that my chance of happiness with him, is as fair, as most people can boast on entering the marriage state'), Lizzy goes to stay at Hunsford Parsonage: 'The garden sloping to the road, the house standing in it, the green pales and the laurel hedge, everything declared they were arriving.' Mr Collins cannot boast of having his own door between the parsonage and the park of Rosings, the residence of Lady Catherine, but he still goes into raptures as he describes the prospect to Elizabeth:

> He could number the fields in every direction, and could tell how many trees there were in the most distant clump. But of all the views which his garden, or which the country, or the kingdom could boast, none were to be compared with the prospect of Rosings, afforded by an opening in the trees that bordered the park nearly opposite the front of his house. It was a handsome,

modern building situated on rising ground.

Later, as they walk across the park to Rosings, after Lady Catherine has condescended to ask them to dine, Elizabeth finds much to admire in the landscape and her view is only slightly affected by Mr Collins's 'enumeration of the windows in the front of the house, and his relation of what the glazing altogether had cost Sir Lewis de Bourgh'.

It's possible that Jane Austen had Godmersham in mind when she wrote these passages. She was composing *Pride and Prejudice* between 1796 and 1797, at about the time that Edward moved his family to Godmersham. Although, as we've seen, she didn't stay there herself until 1798, the house was already well known to her from her earlier visits to Edward and his family at Rowling.

The locations Jane Austen uses in her novels have always excited speculation. The truth is that it's almost always impossible to pin down her inspirations for the great houses of which she writes – Mansfield Park, Pemberley, Northanger Abbey, Kellynch Hall, Hartfield – just as her characters cannot be identified with people she actually knew. They are creations of her imagination, composites of places known to her: in the end they are locations that existed only in her mind's eye.

Nevertheless, her topographical research was meticulous. In January 1813, while she was working on a plot device during the writing of *Mansfield Park*, a novel set 'in the county of Northampton', Jane asked Cassandra to check for her 'whether Northamptonshire is a Country of Hedgerows'. Later, when she was advising her niece Anna on the writing of her own novel in August 1814, she was quick to notice topographical anomalies: 'Lyme will not do. Lyme is towards 40 miles distance from

Dawlish & would not be talked of there'; 'Twice you have put Dorsetshire for Devonshire. I have altered it.'

The producers of the many television and film adaptations of Jane Austen's novels are among those who have scoured their pages in search of location clues. Filming for the BBC's most recent adaptation of *Pride and Prejudice*, first shown in 1995, eventually took place right across England, from Luckington Court in Wiltshire, which became Longbourn, to Lyme Park in Cheshire, which doubled as Pemberley. Belton House in Lincolnshire was used for Rosings. For the film starring Keira Knightley and Matthew Macfadyen, released in 2005, an entirely different set of locations was settled upon: Pemberley was Chatsworth House in Derbyshire; Rosings had switched to Burghley House, also in Lincolnshire; and Groombridge Place, a 17th-century manor house in Kent, became Longbourn. This lack of consensus as to what her locations might have looked like is entirely appropriate.

I admit, however, to being rather pleased when I discovered that Petty France, a real place on the A46 in Gloucestershire, not far from where I live, is mentioned in *Northanger Abbey*, although in less than auspicious terms. En route from Bath to Northanger, Catherine Morland and the Tilneys stop at the coaching inn there:

> The tediousness of a two-hour wait at Petty France, in which there was nothing to be done except eat without being hungry, and loiter about without anything to see, next followed... Had their party been perfectly agreeable, the delay would have been nothing; but General Tilney, though so charming a man, seemed always a check on his children's spirits, and scarcely any thing

was said but by himself; the observation of which, with his discontent at whatever the inn afforded, and his angry impatience at the waiters, made Catherine grow every moment more in awe of him, and appeared to lengthen the two hours into four.

The coaching inn still stands. An attractive 17th-century building, now known as Bodkin House, it features a portrait of Jane Austen on its roadside sign. Its website claims that Jane came here as a child and that on a later visit she is said to have signed one of the first-floor windows with her diamond ring, a popular custom at the time. [8]

'Mr Collins's door' was locked, so I retraced my steps and reentered the park through the wrought iron gates at the top of the Lime Avenue. Rabbits scattered at my approach. Halfway down I turned off to the left, towards Godmersham's newer temple summerhouse, created in the 1930s from the grand portico that originally adorned the south front of the house.

In 1874 Jane's nephew, Edward, who had inherited Godmersham from his father, put the whole estate, including its 15 farms, up for sale. He had made numerous additions to the house after the death of his father in 1832, but had never lived there, preferring instead to reside in the Great House at Chawton in Hampshire. After the estate was sold it experienced several rapid changes of owner and tenant, and deteriorated significantly as a result. In 1933 it was sold again, this time to an art dealer named Robert Tritton. With his American wife Elsie he set about restoring the house with no expense spared, filling it with fine antique furniture from Jane Austen's time. A photograph of the entrance hall that appeared in *Country Life* in 1945 shows the room elegantly furnished with a gilded console table and two handsome embroidered stools. The Trittons also assembled a vast collection of books, many of them about Jane Austen. After Mrs Tritton's death in 1983 the contents of Godmersham were split up and sold at an auction that raised £4 million. The estate was then bought by its current owners, the Sunley family, who, happily, are also sympathetic to its history. Like any large house these days, it must earn its keep, and the tenancy of ABDO had, according to Greg, proved a successful way of doing so.

I sat inside the temple for a while, on a seat placed there in memory of Sir David Waldron Smithers, the first patron of the Kent branch of the Jane Austen Society, which meets regularly at Godmersham. Further down the Lime Walk I came across a scrolled memorial set into the wall in memory of Arthur Thomas Miller, a nephew of the Trittons who was killed in action in Tunisia in March 1945. At the bottom of the Lime Walk, next to the house, are a swimming pool and a tennis court, and a series of pretty walled gardens laid out during the Trittons' time. I wandered around for a while, smelling the roses and losing myself in a maze of topiary. A fountain played in the centre of a white garden, where wooden benches, statues and pots of agapanthus lilies had been placed in secluded corners. Tall spikes of foxglove towered over me as I crunched along the gravel path. It was just the kind of place where you could turn the corner and be surprised by the presence of another person, rather as Elizabeth is at Pemberley when, having been told that Mr Darcy is not at home, she unexpectedly sights him approaching 'at no great distance'.

I called for a taxi to come and pick me up, and sat down to wait on the 17th-century stone bridge, now encrusted with lichen, which crosses the River Stour on the site of an old ford. Weeping willows line the river banks and ducks dabble among the lily pads. It was perfect weather for swimming. In Jane Austen's time there was a bathing house a little further downstream. Swimming and boating were popular summertime activities for all the children at Godmersham. What a glorious place to grow up, I thought.

Half an hour later I sat in a crowded café inside Ashford International Station. As I sipped my tea it was impossible not to overhear the conversation going on between two girls at the table next to me. One of them had been proposed to the previous day by the multiply pierced man talking outside on his mobile phone. Despite not knowing what he was supposed to say on such an occasion ('Hasn't he ever watched the telly?' the other girl asked), he succeeded in asking her to be his wife. That night his new fiancée had scattered their bed with rose petals. 'He was so excited, just like a little kid', she giggled. It transpired that she had thrown a knife at her previous boyfriend, the father of her two children, on discovering that he was being unfaithful, yet she was evidently still embarking on matrimony with admirable enthusiasm.

Godmersham had been a most beguiling destination. Despite being a place where Jane Austen's heritage is largely unexploited, the 'vibes' of her time and milieu had been powerful, and as a result it had captivated me. I was learning too not to go looking for Jane in the obvious places. Perhaps it was better to let her come to me, whether outside a Doric temple on a wooded Kent hillside or in a railway station café. As I left to board my train, I hoped that the rose petal girl would be happy. Perhaps it would be just as Henry Crawford says in *Mansfield Park*: 'An engaged woman is always more agreeable than a disengaged. She is satisfied with herself. Her cares are over.'

Chapter Five
Chawton: 'Home-made'

3 or 4 Families in a Country Village is the very thing to work on. – Letter to Anna Austen, 9–18 September 1814

Chawton. A village so English that you feel you could bottle up its quintessence and take it away. It has a green, a pub, a teashop, a manor house and a church. Thatched cottages nestle down its lanes, their doorways concealed by creepers. Hosts of daffodils and muscari wave from the verges. At the edge of the village the cricket field is set on a crazy incline, its sight screens dazzling white against the dark wood beyond. Leather still thwacks on willow here, a few miles from Hambledon, the Hampshire village where cricket is said to have originated in the mid-18th century.

It was here that Jane Austen spent the last eight years of her life, having willingly embraced the kind of genteel poverty that the heroines of her novels generally manage to avoid. It was back to Hampshire, and to country living after years of town life, most recently in Southampton, where Mrs Austen, Jane, Cassandra and a long-standing family friend, Martha Lloyd, had lived with Frank Austen and his wife after leaving Bath in 1806. Frank and Mary Austen were embarking on family life – the first of their 11 children was born in 1807 – and would soon need more room. The Austen women must surely have been ecstatic at the idea of a permanent home of their own at last. The move to Chawton is mentioned in letters from Jane to Cassandra as early as October 1808, and two months later Jane tells her: 'Every body is much acquainted with Chawton & speaks of it as a remarkably pretty village and every body knows the House we describe – but nobody fixes on the right.'

Jane's brother Edward made the move possible. He was the main landowner in Chawton and, when his bailiff there died, a house, Chawton Cottage, became vacant. Edward's wife Elizabeth had also died during the autumn of 1808, shortly after giving birth to her 11th child. The prospect of having his mother and sisters settled close to one of his country residences must have seemed attractive to a grieving widower with so many children. Edward offered them a choice: a house close to Godmersham, his main residence in Kent, or Chawton Cottage. They chose Chawton. The village was already known to them. It was within walking distance of the shops in Alton, a mile away, where Jane's brother Henry had opened a branch of his bank. Chawton was also only 12 miles or so from their old home at Steventon, where Jane's brother James was now rector, so family get-togethers would be easy to arrange. Though money would still be tight, the Austens would live rent-free and quickly become highly respected members of the village community, as befitted the mother and sisters of the local squire.

Nowadays the word 'cottage' conjures up something small and quaint – perhaps two up, two down, perhaps thatched. In Jane Austen's time a cottage was not necessarily anything so twee. It's a comedown for the Dashwoods in *Sense and Sensibility* when they have to leave Norland Park, their substantial estate in Sussex, for the comparatively modest Barton Cottage in Devon: 'It is but a cottage', Mrs Dashwood says. Yet the house has two sitting rooms, 'offices', four bedrooms and two garrets above.

Built in red brick in the early 18th century, Chawton Cottage, formerly an inn, is also a substantial house. Its six bedrooms provided enough room for the Austens and Martha Lloyd, with space for visitors to stay too. There was also a kitchen garden, a back yard and some outbuildings. Edward had some work done on the house before his mother and sisters moved in, renewing the plumbing and moving a window from the front of the house, with its view of the road, to the side, where to this day it provides a more private aspect over the garden.

In July 1809 Jane, Cassandra, Mrs Austen and Martha were able to move into their new home. Shortly afterwards Frank's wife Mary gave birth to their second child, Francis William, and Jane wrote a congratulatory verse and sent it from Chawton to her brother. It begins: 'My dearest Frank, I wish you joy / Of Mary's safety with a Boy'. In the last stanza she writes of their new home:

> Our Chawton home, how much we find
> Already in it, to our mind;
> And how convinced, that when complete
> It will all other houses beat
> That ever have been made or mended,
> With rooms concise, or rooms distended.
> You'll find us very snug next year ...

I couldn't find a space in the visitors' car park opposite Chawton Cottage, so I parked down by the cricket field. A match was in progress, and the players' wives and girlfriends were busy buttering bread in the thatched pavilion. Someone struck a boundary up the hill and the ball rolled helpfully back down the slope into the hands of the defeated fielder. Nearby a group of local youths in grey hoodies had plonked themselves miserably in the deep shade of a tree. A poster on a nearby telegraph pole pleaded for news of Aggie, a lost Norwegian Forest Cat, while lawnmowers at work all around the village provided an ambient hum.

In the middle of the village a black-and-white sign points one of its outstretched arms at Chawton Cottage. Behind the house two ancient yew trees spread their branches darkly across the sky, dwarfing the house below. On the front wall a memorial commemorates the purchase of Chawton Cottage by Thomas Edward Carpenter, a JP of Mill Hill in London, in memory of his son, Lieutenant Philip John Carpenter of the East Surrey Regiment, who was killed in action at Lake Trasimene in Italy in 1944. Carpenter founded the Jane Austen Memorial Trust, which now owns and administers the house, first opened as a museum in 1949.

Chawton today should be a drowsy place. The busy A31 bypasses the village on its way from Winchester to Farnham, and if it were not for the Jane Austen connection, there would be little reason to stop off here at all. In the early 19th century, however, Chawton was at an important fork in the turnpike road from London. Coaches regularly rattled through the village on their way to Alton and London to the north, or back towards Winchester or Gosport to the west and south. Unlike Jane's previous Hampshire home, buried in sleepy Steventon, Chawton Cottage, right on the road, was a place where you could sit and watch the world go by, and the world could watch you too. Not long after Jane moved to the Cottage, a gentleman of Mrs Knight's acquaintance who was travelling past the Austens' door in a Post-chaise reported catching a glimpse of the Chawton party sitting very comfortably at their breakfast.

Pass by the same window today on your way round to the entrance of Chawton Cottage and you can snoop in on the same modest dining parlour. It has a low ceiling, daintily papered walls and a polished wooden floor. A copper kettle sits in the fireplace. (It once belonged, not to the Austens, but to the illustrator Kate Greenaway.) The dining table is set with white china and family miniatures gaze down from above the mantelpiece. All that is missing are the women of the house, drinking their morning tea and discussing the day ahead.

I paid for my ticket at the desk in the drawing room. In the middle of the room a table was set with souvenirs: fridge magnets, feather-topped biros posing as quill pens and 'top quality' leather mousemats. There are few other intrusions from the 21st century. The house is charmingly modest. Its floors slope, its floorboards squeak. Little vases of flowers have been set lovingly in every room. Delicately placed fir cones and lavender stems have been laid on the chairs, instead of stern notices, to stop you sitting down and making yourself at home, as you long to.

It was a May Bank Holiday weekend and the Cottage was full of visitors. We creaked our way from room to room, squeezing ever so politely round one another, to look at the exhibits. Behind me a man yawned discreetly in his wife's wake.

An air of homely simplicity has been artfully preserved at Chawton Cottage: you search each austere corner in vain for anything that might have sent Jane's imagination soaring as she composed the three novels she wrote here. Her earliest surviving letters from Chawton, written in late May 1811, dwell rather charmingly on the domestic. When Cassandra was away Jane was left in charge of the house and garden, and kept her sister appraised of all the latest developments: 'The Chicken are all alive, & fit for the Table – but we save them for something grand. The flower seeds are coming up but your Mignonette makes a wretched appearance.' A couple of days later she wrote: 'I will not say that your Mulberry Trees are dead, but I am afraid they are not alive'; then she added better news: 'We shall have pease soon – I mean to have them with a couple of Ducks.' In a spirit of friendly competition neighbours in villages all over England vied with one another each summer to have the first crop of green peas ready for the king's birthday on 4 June.

In the drawing room there is a piano built in 1810, similar to the one that Jane played here each morning before breakfast. A copy of Clementi's *Sonatina*, Opus 30, no. 1, is propped open at the ready. Before the move here from Southampton Jane had written in December 1808: 'Yes, yes we will have a Pianoforte, as good a one as can be get for 30 guineas – and I will practice country dances, that we may have some amusement for our nephews and nieces when we have the pleasure of their company.' Nearby is a handsome Hepplewhite bureau bookcase that once belonged to George Austen, now crammed with old editions of Jane's novels, including copies of the first American editions, published in the 1830s. It struck me with a pang that the father who had so encouraged his daughter in her early attempts at writing did not live to see any of her work in print.

It was in this beamed room that Jane, Cassandra, their mother and Martha entertained visitors, or sat sewing, drawing or reading aloud from the latest novel after an early dinner. Standing there, watching the comings and goings of visitors, I found it difficult to conjure up a vision of the scene: there isn't even a sofa. Then again, even Jane Austen's imagination might have been defeated if you had asked her to picture her sitting room with a till in one corner, a table of souvenirs bearing her own silhouette in the centre and a constant stream of visitors coming in through a front door that didn't even exist in her day.

Across the vestibule a now redundant corridor that in Jane's time was the main entrance hall, is the dining room, its table set with the Wedgwood dinner service mentioned in a letter written to Cassandra at Chawton in September 1813. At the time Jane was staying in London with her brother Henry and three of her nieces from Godmersham. After the girls had endured a painful trip to the dentist they went shopping at Wedgwood's in York Street, where Jane's eldest niece Fanny and her father Edward chose a 'Dinner Set'. Jane told Cassandra: 'I beleive [*sic*] the pattern is a small Lozenge in purple, between Lines of narrow Gold; – & it is to have the Crest.'

Breakfast at Chawton was taken at around nine o'clock, after some of the day's errands and chores were out of the way. It was usually Jane herself who unlocked the cupboard by the fireplace, took out the precious tea, boiled water in the kettle and prepared breakfast. According to the website of the Jane Austen Centre in Bath, this consisted of tea, toast, pound cake and, occasionally, cocoa. [1] For the rest of the day Cassandra took charge of the housekeeping, leaving Jane free to write. It was here in this same room that she composed the three novels she wrote while living at Chawton: *Mansfield Park*, *Emma* and *Persuasion*.

Writers these days are usually pretty particular about their working conditions. A room of one's own (in Virginia Woolf's phrase) is usually felt to be essential. They have fetishes for materials, with particular brands of stationery or pens often assuming totemic importance. If their domestic surroundings cease to be sufficiently inspiring, there are writers' retreats, where they can compare notes with other writers, or let off steam about their frustrations; there are writing circles and writing organizations to provide support.

Jane Austen had none of these things. In his *Memoir of Jane Austen* her nephew, James Edward Austen-Leigh, acknowledged that she 'lived in entire seclusion from the literary world... It is probable that she never was in company with any persons whose talents or whose celebrity equalled her own; so that her powers never could have been sharpened by collision with superior intellects, nor her imagination aided by their casual suggestions. Whatever she produced was a home-made article.'[2]

So it was in seclusion in this room that Jane wrote and revised her 'home-made articles'. Unlike almost every floorboard, the squeaky door, which was never repaired, so that she could tell when someone was coming and slide her writings out of sight, seems to squeak no longer (I tried it). Aside from groaning doors and floorboards, the dining room would probably have been one of the noisiest rooms in which she could choose to work, and it was certainly not private. Along the turnpike road, right outside the window, came the coaches: two a day from Winchester and one at midday from Portsmouth. The local collier's coach, drawn by six horses, passed once a day from Alton. Farmers' carts, gigs and occasional grand private carriages added to the traffic. One of Jane's letters from Chawton written in July

1816, mentions that she saw 'a countless numbers of Postchaises full of Boys pass by yesterday morning – full of future Heroes, Legislators, Fools, & Vilains'. These were schoolboys on their way to Winchester College, the alma mater of James Edward Austen-Leigh and all of Jane's Kent nephews.

By the dining-room window there is a small three-legged table, no more than three feet high, with an uneven surface. It looks like the kind of table that someone might set a pewter mug of ale on to drink by the fireside. It was on this inadequate-looking table that Jane set her writing desk, possibly the one that her father bought for her in 1794, and worked on her novels, in full view of the road. After Jane's death Cassandra gave the table to an elderly servant for his cottage: it was bought back by the Knight family from the man's grandson in 1913. After a visit to Chawton in 1969 the novelist Barbara Pym wrote in her diary: 'I put my hand down on Jane's desk and bring it up covered with dust... One would have imagined the devoted female custodian going round with her duster at least every other day.'[3]

I didn't detect any dust, but I longed to sit at the table and try it out. The practicalities suddenly confounded me. How could she have got comfortable enough to write even a short letter at such a table? It seemed even more remarkable to think that all her novels were written, not only in long hand, but also with a quill pen. Steel pen nibs were not invented until the 1830s. If you've ever tried to use a quill, you'll know that they splay out with use and have to be trimmed back into shape regularly with a penknife (hence the name, of course). No wonder Jane Austen famously wrote of 'the little bit, (two inches wide) of ivory on which I work with so fine a brush as produces little effect after much labour'. Jane often remarks on Cassandra's 'fine hand', envying her ability to squeeze so much onto one sheet of paper (postage costs increased with the number of pages used): 'You are very clever to write such long Letters; every page of yours has more lines than this, & every line more words than the average of mine… I am sick of myself, & my bad pens', she wrote in June 1808. On another occasion, in November 1813, when her pen 'seems inclined to write large', Jane wrote: 'The day seems to improve. I wish my pen would too.'

James Edward Austen-Leigh wrote in his *Memoir* that: 'I have no doubt that I, and my sisters and cousins, in our visits to Chawton, frequently disturbed this mystic process, without having any idea of the mischief we were doing.'[4] It's possible, of course, that Jane found the traffic noise and the comings and goings outside stimulating rather than distracting, but the conditions under which she worked would probably thwart many writers today, used as they generally are to the luxury of desks, ergonomic chairs and word processors. Yet the only thing Jane ever complained about, at least so far as we know from her surviving letters, was the difficulty of concentrating on her work while trying to run a household at the same time: 'Composition seems to me Impossible with a head full of Joints of Mutton & doses of Rhubarb', she wrote in September 1816.

Domestic headaches did not prevent Jane from getting down to some serious work very soon after settling at Chawton, however. In the summer of 1809 she took out the manuscript of *Sense and Sensibility*, which she had last worked on in 1798. The book, originally written in the form of letters, and entitled *Elinor and Marianne*, had already been completely revised once. Now, more than ten years later, Jane made some additional small changes to the novel in order to update it. Deirdre Le Faye identifies them in *Jane Austen: The World of Her Novels*: the smart barouche in which Mrs Palmer is driven about was not known in England until 1800; the twopenny post by means of which Marianne daringly sends a letter to Willoughby (single women were not supposed to correspond with men unless they were engaged) did not cost two pennies until 1801; and Sir Walter Scott, whose verse Marianne discusses with Willoughby, became widely known only after the publication of *The Lay of the Last Minstrel* in 1805.[5]

Jane was an admirer of Scott's work. After he began to publish novels, in September 1814, she wrote to Cassandra: 'Walter Scott has no business to write novels, especially good ones. – It is not fair. – He has Fame and Profit enough as a Poet, and should not be taking the bread out of other people's mouths. – I do not like him, & do not mean to like *Waverley* if I can help it but fear I must.' In his turn Scott was rather condescending about Jane's work during her lifetime, perhaps the reason for her dislike, but after her death he seems to have revised his opinion, declaring: 'That lady has a talent for describing the involvements and feelings and characters of ordinary life, which to me is the most wonderful I have ever met with. The Big Bow-Wow strain I can do myself like any now going; but the exquisite touch which renders ordinary common-place things interesting from the truth of the description and the sentiment is denied to me.'[6]

Something, or someone, must have encouraged Jane to revisit *Sense and Sensibility* in order to prepare it for submission to a publisher. Her only previous attempt at publication had been in 1797, when her father sent *First Impressions*, the early version of *Pride and Prejudice*, to Thomas Cadell, a well-known

London publisher, accompanied by a letter that scarcely did it justice. It was declined by return of post. We have no way of knowing how much this rejection may have discouraged Jane, if indeed it did. By the time she was living at Chawton, George Austen had been dead for almost five years and her brother Henry had taken over his father's role as Jane's literary mentor. Henry, who was much better informed about such matters, sent *Sense and Sensibility* to Thomas Egerton of Whitehall in 1810. Egerton agreed to publish the book, but only on commission, meaning that the author had to cover the costs of printing it, and contribute towards advertising and distribution costs as well, whilst Egerton would retain the copyright. Henry and his wife Eliza footed the bill, and, after a considerable delay, *Sense and Sensibility* was finally published in October 1811, as a 'New Novel by a Lady'.

About 1,000 copies of the book were printed, with a purchase price of 15 shillings for the three-volume set. It soon attracted the attention of the great and the good. Even the 16-year-old heir to the throne, Princess Charlotte, read it, remarking that it 'interested me much'. By the summer of 1813 the first run had sold out, making Jane a profit of £140 (equivalent to about £9,000 today). At last she was a published writer, albeit anonymously so, and earning her own money for the first time in her life. With the delight of seeing her work in print must have come the delicious sensation that her days of total economic dependence on her brothers were at an end. It was a vindication too of her decision to sacrifice everything – marriage, children and material wealth – in order to write. What a time to savour. As Fay Weldon once wrote: 'Pity Jane Austen if you must, this maiden lady without children or sexual experience. But she would have known the exhilaration of the writer when she put down her pen after *Pride and Prejudice*. I bet she knew that what she'd written would outrun the generations.'[7]

.There was no longer any need for Jane to dwell on the subject of marriage outside her novels, except perhaps in jest. A running family joke throughout the Chawton years was the eligible bachelor status of Mr Papillon, the village rector, who lived with his sister at the rectory beside Chawton Great House. When the move to Chawton was first spoken of in December 1808, Edward Knight's adoptive mother, Mrs Knight, of whom Jane was rather fond, homed in on Mr Papillon as a potential husband for her and Jane joked at the time: 'She may depend on it, I will marry Mr Papillon, whatever may be his reluctance, or my own.' The fun at Mr Papillon's expense continued for years. As late as December 1816 Jane wrote to James Edward: 'I am happy to tell you that Mr Papillon will soon make his offer.' Something must have made him wildly unsuitable to be the butt of such mischief. All we have from Jane is her comment after an evening gathering at the Papillons in January 1813 that a 'better Master of the House' was wanting, 'one less anxious & fidgetty [*sic*], & more conversible'.

Next Jane revised the manuscript of *Pride and Prejudice* and, in the autumn of 1812, Thomas Egerton offered to buy the copyright. In November Jane wrote to Martha Lloyd, who was staying with friends in Berkshire, to tell her: 'Egerton gives £110 for it. – I would rather have had £150, but we could not both be pleased, and I am not at all surprised that he should not chuse to hazard so much.' Early in 1813 it followed *Sense and*

Sensibility into print. She had a completed copy in her hand by the end of January and wrote to Cassandra: 'I want to tell you that I have got my own darling Child from London. The Advertisement is in our paper to day for the first time; – 18s – He shall ask £1-1 for my two next, & £1-8 for my stupidest of all.'

It was *Pride and Prejudice* that came to mind as I creaked my way up the stairs at Chawton: on the door to the bookshop below me someone had stuck a photograph of Colin Firth in his seminal role as Mr Darcy in the BBC's adaptation, back in 1995. Ever since the first transmission of the episode in which he takes off his shirt and dives into the lake at Pemberley (an incident that does not happen in the book, of course) legions of women have swooned over Firth, including Bridget Jones, for whom Helen Fielding created the character of Mark Darcy. The *Radio Times* even printed a pull-out pin-up poster of Firth in the role, which, ten years later, is still Blu-Tacked to the inside of one of my mother-in-law's kitchen cupboards as well as to the door at Chawton.

Firth almost turned the part of Mr Darcy down and had to be talked into taking it. In Penguin's bestselling tie-in book, *The Making of Pride and Prejudice*, there is a long interview with him: 'I didn't feel right for Darcy. I looked in the mirror and I didn't see him. And then my brother [Jonathan, also an actor,] said, "Darcy, isn't he supposed to be sexy?"'

In fact, Colin Firth was almost too sexy as Darcy. His performance induced weak knees all over Britain, and prompted my mother and me to wonder, laughingly, what possible objections Elizabeth could possibly have to marrying him. He was impossibly rich, impossibly handsome and a bit 'up himself' perhaps, but what's your problem, woman? I've wound up lots of friends by suggesting that it is Elizabeth's visit to Pemberley that is really responsible for changing her mind about Mr Darcy. Having viewed the magnificent house and its extensive grounds, she decides that she really quite likes him after all.

Jane was, of course, very attached to her heroine, Elizabeth. She wrote from Chawton in January 1813: 'I must confess that I think her as delightful creature as ever appeared in print, & how I shall be able to tolerate those who do not like her at least, I do not know.'

On the way up the stairs I squeezed past a couple of people standing by a pot plant on the small first landing, queuing for the loo. When I went in there later I decided that it was in want of a chintzy curtain: I had to duck down below the bare window to be out of sight of some cyclists chatting in the back yard.

At the top of the stairs the first bedroom on the right is the one that belonged to Jane and Cassandra. Unlike in all their previous homes, there were enough bedrooms at Chawton Cottage for each of the Austen women to have a room to herself, but Jane and Cassandra chose to share as they had always done. Much enjoyable end-of-day gossip must have passed between them as they got ready for bed and, when their niece Anna sent Jane her own novel in progress in September 1814, Jane wrote back to her: 'I have read it to your Aunt Cassandra… in our own room at night, while we undressed.' It seems a small room for two people to share. To allow room for visitors, there is no longer even a bed in it.

Among the many exhibits framed on the wall of the room is

an extract from Sir Winston Churchill's *The Second World War* in which he recalls reading *Pride and Prejudice* while suffering from pneumonia at the height of the conflict: 'What calm lives they had, these people! No worries about the French Revolution, or the crashing struggle of the Napoleonic Wars.'[8] It's true that events in the outside world rarely intrude into Jane's novels, but it seems pointless to criticize her for the fact. The novelist David Lodge got it right when he wrote that Jane 'was a great writer. It is easy to mistake what is exotic and unfamiliar for real originality.'[9] Another novelist, Elizabeth Bowen, put it even better: 'she dispels, except for the very stupid, the fallacy that life with the lid off – in thieves' kitchens, prisons, taverns and brothels – is necessarily more interesting than life with the lid on'.[10]

In any case, Jane's letters reveal that she was all too aware of world events. The Chawton years were turbulent ones for the nation, witnessing the Luddite riots, the introduction of the Corn Laws, the political turmoil of the Regency period and, of course, the Napoleonic Wars. In a letter of 31 May 1811 Jane refers to the Battle of Albuera, one of many bloody exchanges between the French and the Allied force of British, Spanish, and Portuguese troops during the Peninsular Wars (the French were defeated, but the British sustained heavy casualties): 'How horrible it is to have so many people killed! – And what a blessing that one cares for none of them!'

Jane knew only too well what it was to care about relatives serving abroad. Along the first-floor landing is the 'Admirals' Room', a bedroom now dedicated to Jane's two sailor brothers. One of them, Francis Austen, rose to the rank of admiral of the Fleet and was knighted by King William IV. Among the items on display is his portable cabin bed, which he took on all his voyages. Much to his chagrin, Frank managed to miss the Battle of Trafalgar, as he was at sea elsewhere. The other, Charles Austen, became a rear admiral, serving in North American waters and later in the Far East, where he died of cholera while on active service in 1852. Downstairs in the vestibule there is a display drawer containing two beautiful topaz crosses that Charles bought for his sisters with prize money awarded for his capture of a French vessel in 1801. Jane, apparently trying hard to be cross with him, wrote to Cassandra in May of that year: 'What avail is it to take prizes if he lays out the Produce in presents to his Sisters... he must be well scolded.' Years later, when she came to write *Mansfield Park*, Jane had William Price, Fanny's sailor brother, make his sister a present of an amber cross. Indeed, *Mansfield Park* is something of a tribute to both her sailor brothers. In a letter of July 1813 Jane wrote to Frank: 'I have something in hand, which I hope on the credit of P.&P. will sell well, tho' not half so entertaining. And by the bye – shall you object to my mentioning the Elephant in it, & two or three other of your old Ships?'

At first only Jane's immediate family shared the closely guarded secret of her authorship. Her identity remained a mystery to her public. Once her first two novels had received a good critical reception, however, Jane seems to have become more relaxed, as word spread as to the identity of the author of *Pride and Prejudice*, and she suggested to Cassandra that she prepare herself for 'the Neighbourhood perhaps being already informed of there being such a Work in the World, & in the Chawton World!' By September 1813 the secret was clearly out. Jane wrote to Cassandra from Godmersham: 'I beleive [*sic*] whenever the 3rd appears, I shall not even attempt to tell Lies about it – I shall rather try to make all the Money than all the Mystery I can of it. People shall pay for their Knowledge if I can make them.' Jane's nephew James Edward composed the following verse in her honour when he realized his aunt was famous:

No words can express, my dear aunt, my surprise
Or make you conceive how I opened my eyes,
Like a pig butcher Pile has just stuck with a knife,
When I heard for the very first time in my life
That I had the honour to have a relation,
Whose works were dispersed through the whole of the nation.

During the early part of 1813 Jane spent many a happy evening with her mother, her sister and a neighbour, Miss Benn, taking turns in reading *Pride and Prejudice* aloud. Whether Miss Benn was in on the secret of the book's authorship isn't clear, but she seems to have enjoyed it immensely, despite Jane being less than satisfied with her mother's attempts at speaking the characters. 'She was amused, poor soul!', writes Jane in January 1813 of Miss Benn, for whom such evenings must have been a rare treat. In her late 40s, she was the genteel but impoverished and unmarried sister of a clergyman who lived in a neighbouring village. He had 11 children to support, so presumably he could do little or nothing for his sister. The Austens took Miss Benn under their wing and Jane, who was so frequently rude about people, seems to have regarded her with nothing but compassion. She may even have thought, on occasion: there but for my own brothers, and now my writing, go I.

Miss Benn lived across the road from Chawton Cottage in a

house called The Thatches, now a very desirable property of the kind that prompts estate agents to reel off a stream of country cottage clichés. Around the time that she was enjoying the evening readings of *Pride and Prejudice* Miss Benn heard that she was to be evicted from her house. As Jane put it in February 1813: 'She will have 3 months before her – & if anything else can be met with, she will be glad enough to be driven from her present wretched abode; – it has been terrible for her during the late storms of wind & rain.' It's possible that Jane had Miss Benn in her mind when she created the character of Miss Bates in *Emma*: 'Her youth had passed without distinction and her middle of life was devoted to the care of a failing mother, and the endeavour to make a small income go as far as possible. And yet she was a happy woman, and a woman whom no one named without good-will.' Miss Benn died in early 1816, at the age of 49.

Miss Benn could have claimed one priceless stroke of good fortune in her life: that of hearing *Pride and Prejudice* read aloud by its author. How much would a literary festival-goer pay for the privilege today? It has always been the most popular of Jane Austen's novels and is available today in over 40 languages. Some of these foreign editions now grace the mantelpiece in Jane's former bedroom. The Czech edition is invitingly entitled *Pýcha a Předsudek*, its author's name rendered as 'Jane Austenová'.

Mansfield Park, the first entire novel Jane wrote while she was living at Chawton, was completed in late 1813 and published in May 1814, priced at 18 shillings for the three volumes. Jane's publisher, Thomas Egerton, was less enthused by it than he had been by *Pride and Prejudice*, and did not offer to buy the copy-right. The novel was therefore published on commission, and advertised as 'by the author of *Sense and Sensibility* and *Pride and Prejudice*'. No reviews appeared, but the novel sold reason-ably well and by November 1814 Jane was able to write to her niece Fanny that the 'first Edit: of M.P. is all sold'. She made up for the lack of reviews by recording the opinions of friends and relations. Most were complimentary, but their praise was gener-ally more muted than that which had been showered on *Pride and Prejudice*. Frank said that although he 'did not think it as a whole equal to P&P', it still had 'many & great beauties'. One wonders if he sniggered at Mary Crawford's remark about her acquaintance with a 'circle of admirals': 'Of Rears and Vices, I saw enough. Now, do not be suspecting me of a pun, I entreat.' Among the characters in the novel he seems to have preferred Aunt Norris, who, he declared, was 'a great favourite' with him.

While I was reading one of the Harry Potter books to my son shortly after my visit to Chawton I found myself wondering whether J.K. Rowling had had Mrs Norris from *Mansfield Park* in mind when she named the malevolent cat belonging to Filch, the caretaker at Hogwarts. After all, both are sly creatures who sneak up on wrongdoers and loudly proclaim their guilt. Jane's Mrs Norris prowls by day, scolding Fanny for such offences as sitting down: 'Take my word for it, it is a shocking trick for a young person to be always lolling upon a sofa.' Jane seems to have allowed herself no such indulgences at Chawton. The one sofa in the house remained very much Mrs Austen's domain. When Jane became ill in 1816 and needed to lie down increasingly often while downstairs, she still wouldn't use the sofa, but constructed a makeshift one for herself from three chairs. Caroline Austen wrote in her memoir, *My Aunt Jane Austen*, published in 1867:

> I wondered, and wondered – for the real sofa was frequently vacant, and still she laid in this comfortless manner. I often asked her how she could like the chairs best – and I suppose I worried her into telling me the reason of her choice – which was, that if she ever used the sofa, Grandmamma would be leaving it for her, and would not lie down, as she did now, whenever she felt inclined.[11]

Mrs Austen occupied the largest bedroom at Chawton Cottage. Spacious it may have been, but with its window at the front of the house it can't have been very quiet. Caroline Austen recalled that 'most delightful it was to a child to have the awful stillness of the night so frequently broken by the noise of passing carriages which seemed sometimes even to shake the bed'.[12] As you enter the room today an accomplished watercolour by Cassandra, depicting a hunter in a landscape, hangs on the blue spriggy papered walls, along with a portrait of Jane and Cassandra's nephew Edward Knight, who lived at Chawton Great House from 1826. He subsequently became the first chairman of the company that laid the railway from Alton to Winchester. The line is no longer part of the passenger network, but it is still used by the steam trains of the Mid Hants Railway. A tour of Chawton Cottage today is likely to be punctuated by the whistles of steam locomotives, chuffing along the so-called Watercress Line in the distance.

Many interesting family objects are on display in Mrs Austen's room: satin slippers, a needlecase made by Jane, a snuffbox, an engagement ring. There are also some toys that look impossibly delicate by today's sturdy plastic standards: spillikins made of whalebone, ivory and wooden dolls, and an ivory cup and ball. Jane was a dab hand at such games, according to her nephew James Edward: 'None of us could throw spillikins in so perfect a circle, or take them off with so steady a hand. Her performances with cup and ball were marvellous.'[13]

Moving round the glass cases, I stopped to stare in awed fascination at a mourning brooch containing a coil of Jane's hair. I had often seen such jewellery at antique fairs, passing over it with a vague shudder at the seeming morbidness of the Victorians, yet in Jane Austen's time too a lock of hair was a souvenir of the dead, to be treasured. After Jane's death Cassandra cut off several locks of her hair as keepsakes.

Jokes and apparent flippancy about death, even about murder, are a speciality of Jane's, especially in her letters: 'Kill poor Mrs Sclater if you like it, while you are at Manydown', she exhorts Cassandra in February 1813 (it's unclear what Mrs Sclater had done to deserve such a fate); 'Sir Thomas Miller is dead. I treat you with a dead Baronet in almost every Letter' (this is in September 1816). And in October 1813, 'Only think of Mrs Holder's being dead! – Poor woman, she has done the only thing in the World she could possibly do, to make one cease to abuse her.' Doctors and nurses are notoriously expert at graveyard humour today, but in the early 19th century, when bereavement was certainly a regular feature of life, perhaps such humour was more widespread. While Jane was living at Chawton, the wives of two of her brothers died. Eliza, Henry's wife, succumbed to cancer and then Charles's wife, Fanny, died, aged 24, giving birth to their fourth child. She became Jane's fourth and youngest dead sister-in-law. Frank Austen was also later to lose his wife in childbirth. The baby was their 11th child and did not live either.

Plenty of nephews and nieces did survive, however. Between them four of Jane's brothers had a total of 33 children, all but nine of them born in her lifetime. Jane had fulfilled the role of affectionate aunt since she was 20 and James's daughter Anna had come to live at Steventon for a while after the death of her mother in 1795. Jane remained close to Anna for the rest of her life. In her early 20s Anna began to write a novel. Jane encouraged her, made suggestions, and read the manuscript aloud to her mother and Cassandra, writing in July 1814 that: 'It has entertained me extremely, all of us indeed.' She was quite specific in her advice, writing, for example, that two of Anna's characters 'must be two days going from Dawlish to Bath. They are nearly 100 miles apart.' She picked up on clichés: 'I wish you would not let him plunge into a "vortex of Dissipation". I do not object to the Thing, but I cannot bear the expression; – it is such a thorough novel slang and so old, that I dare say Adam met with it in the first novel he opened.' There was also her famous advice about three or four families in a country village: 'You are now collecting your People delightfully, getting them exactly into such a spot as is the delight of my life.'

In November 1814, Anna married Ben Lefroy, a relative of Jane's old flame Tom. She gave birth to two daughters within a year of one another, and seems to have had less time for writing after that. In a letter to Anna's half-sister, Caroline Austen, shortly after the birth of Anna's first child, Anna Jemima, in October 1815, Jane wrote: 'Now that you are become an Aunt you are a person of some consequence & must excite great Interest whatever You do. I have always maintained the importance of Aunts as much as possible.' By this time ten-year-old Caroline was also writing a novel and her aunt was soon dispensing authorial advice once again.

Following the death of their mother, Elizabeth, in 1808, Jane's nephews Edward, aged 14, and George, aged 12, came to stay with her for a while in Southampton. She comforted them, and distracted them from their grief by playing cup and ball, spillikins, and card games with them, making paper ships, and going for walks with them along the river. In October 1808, she wrote to Cassandra, who was staying at Godmersham to help to look after the younger motherless Austen Knight siblings: 'While I write now, George is most industriously making and naming paper ships, at which he afterwards shoots with horse chestnuts.' Meanwhile Edward was reading a novel and 'twisting himself about in one of our great chairs'. Their younger sisters, Lizzy, aged eight, and Marianne, aged seven, did not get to play cup and ball with their aunt, but were dispatched to boarding school in Essex for a few months until a governess could be found for them. A charming miniature of the two sisters, aged five and four, is on display at Chawton Cottage, their little faces innocently unaware of the sad blow that fate was shortly to deal them.

In later years the floorboards at Chawton Cottage often resounded to the clatter of small feet when Jane's younger nephews and nieces, the children of her brothers Frank and

Charles, came to visit. Charles's daughters, Cassandra (known as Cassy) and Harriet, regularly stayed with their aunts at Chawton, particularly after the death of their mother in 1814. Jane clearly took great pleasure in their company, but found their behaviour lacking at times: 'Charles' little girls were with us about a month & had so endeared themselves that we were quite sorry to have them go. We have the pleasure however of hearing that they are thought very much improved at home – Harriet in health, Cassy in manners. The latter ought to be a very nice child ... but Method has been wanting', she wrote in July 1813. Her remarks about a badly behaved nephew of Anna's husband, Ben, show that she was a bit of stickler of the 'spare the rod' variety: 'We thought him a very fine boy, but terribly in want of Discipline. – I hope he gets a wholesome thump, or two whenever it is necessary', she wrote in July 1815. Frank's children also seem to have needed reining in: 'the children are sometimes very noisy & not under such Order as they ought & easily might', she remarked to Caroline in January 1817. Yet she could not 'help liking them & even loving them, which I hope may be not wholly inexcusable in their & your affectionate Aunt'. A lovely conundrum letter to eight year-old Cassy, written at the turn of Jane's last year, survives. 'Ym raed Yssac', it begins. 'I hsiw uoy a yppah wen raey,' and it ends: 'Ryou Etanoitceffa Tnua, Enaj Netsua'.

It was to Fanny Austen Knight, Edward's eldest daughter, that she wrote her most moving and revealing 'Aunt Jane' letters. Jane had once written of Fanny (in Ocotber 1808) that she was 'almost another Sister... [I] could not have supposed that a neice [*sic*] would ever have been so much to me.' The eldest of 11 children, Fanny was 15 when her mother died and consequently spent a great deal of time during her formative years playing the role of surrogate mother. When she reached an age to consider marriage for herself, Fanny was riddled with doubts about how to recognize the right man when she saw him. In 1814 she almost became engaged to the rich and eligible John Plumptre, but something held her back. In November of that year, Aunt Jane tried to help her niece to gauge her true feelings. On the one hand, 'There are such beings in the World perhaps, one in a Thousand, as the Creature You & I should think perfection, where Grace & Spirit are united to Worth, where the manners are equal to the Heart & Understanding, but such a person may not come in your way, or if he does, he may not be the eldest son of a Man of Fortune, the Brother of your particular friend, & belonging to your own County. – Think of all this Fanny. Mr JP has advantages which do not often meet in one person.' Is this the woman who turned down Harris Bigg-Wither?

She is indeed that woman, as becomes clear just a few lines later, when she turns powerful Devil's advocate. 'And now, my dear Fanny, having written so much on one side of the question, I shall turn round & entreat you not to commit yourself farther, & not to think of accepting him unless you really do like him. Anything is to be preferred or endured rather than marrying without Affection.' She assures Fanny that John Plumptre will get over it: 'It is no creed of mine, as you must be well aware, that such sort of Disappointments kill anybody.'

Fanny did not marry John Plumptre. A few months before her death, in March 1817, Jane wrote another letter to her favourite niece: 'Do not be in a hurry; depend upon it, the right Man will come at last; you will in the course of the next two or three years, meet with somebody more generally unexceptionable than anyone you have yet known, who will love you as warmly as ever He did, & who will so completely attach you that will feel you never really loved before.' In 1820 Fanny met and married Sir Edward Knatchbull, a rich widower baronet with six children. A surrogate mother once more, Fanny went on to have nine children of her own. Perhaps it was fitting that Jane did not live to see this much-loved contrary niece married. One of the last of Jane's letters among those that have survived was written to Fanny on 20 February 1817: 'Who can keep pace with the fluctuations of your Fancy, the Capprizios of your Taste, the Contradictions of your Feelings?... Oh! what a loss it will be, when you are married. You are too agreeable in your single state. Too agreeable as a Neice [*sic*]. I shall hate you when your delicious play of Mind is all settled down into conjugal and maternal affections... And yet I do wish you to marry very much, because I know you will never be happy till you are; but the loss of a Fanny Knight will be never made up to me.' She seems to have written that passage only half in jest. This is one of my favourite Austen letters, because the feelings of the writer, so often held in check, burst from the page.

Also on display in Mrs Austen's bedroom is Martha Lloyd's Household Book. I read through her recipes for rice pudding, Scotch collops (a dish made with veal) and a method for making 'Balls' with suet. There are also instructions on how to 'stew Piggeons brown'. Seasonal food is very much in vogue these days, partly as a reaction against the insatiable but environmentally questionable year-round demand for commodities such as salad and strawberries. In the early 19th century, however, it was not a matter of fashions or fads: almost all food was still produced locally, and its availability was totally dependent on the weather and the seasons. Waste not, want not was the maxim, and every last cut of meat made its appearance on the dinner table – udders, testicles, pigs' ears, cocks' combs. Jane once wrote (in November 1798): 'I am very fond of experimental housekeeping, such as having an ox-cheek now and then.' The more a household could grow or produce for itself, the better. Jane's letters from Chawton contain many references to home-grown produce, which was consumed fresh, bottled, pickled, fermented or brewed. Thus, in May 1811: 'We are likely to have a great crop of Orleans plumbs – but not many greengages'; then in June: 'Yesterday I had the agreeable surprise of finding several scarlet strawberries quite ripe... There are more Gooseberries & fewer Currants than I thought at first. – We must buy Currants for our Wine'; in September: 'We must husband our present stock of Mead; – and I am sorry to perceive that our 20 Gal; [gallons] is very nearly out'; and in December: 'The Pickled Cucumbers are extremely good.' Gifts from her brothers were recorded appreciatively: a stilton cheese from Henry, pork from James at Steventon, a ham from Edward at Chawton Great House and free firewood from the estate.

Emma was written between January 1814, and March 1815, in between making visits to London to see Henry, looking after a constant stream of visiting relatives at Chawton and dispensing advice to her two oldest nieces. After Egerton had refused to bring out a second edition of *Mansfield Park,* Jane had acquired a new publisher, John Murray. *Emma* came out early in 1816, with a dedication to the Prince Regent. After the muted reception for *Mansfield Park*, Jane was worried about what her audience would make of her latest novel, as a letter written to James Stanier Clarke, the Prince's librarian, in December 1815 reveals: 'My greatest anxiety at present is that this 4th work should not disgrace what was good in the others. But on this point I will do myself the justice to declare that whatever may be my wishes for its' [*sic*] success, I am very strongly haunted by the idea that to those Readers who have preferred P&P it will appear inferior in Wit, & to those who have preferred MP very inferior in good Sense. Such as it is however, I hope you will do me the favour of accepting a Copy.' Most of Jane's friends and relatives, including her mother, do indeed seem to have preferred *Pride and Prejudice*, and it remains her most popular novel today. When he read *Emma*, Jane's nephew Edward pointed out a rare example of what might now be called a continuity error: his aunt had made Mr Knightley's apple trees blossom in July. Nevertheless, many critics regard *Emma* as Jane's most accomplished novel.

Back downstairs once again, past Colin Firth's glowering Darcy, the shop at Chawton Cottage offers visitors a tempting range of Austenalia, from books and videos to framed silhouettes, teatowels, peg-bags and needlepoint kits. However, even the most dedicated of seamstresses would be hard pressed to match the precise beauty of the patchwork quilt draped over an old four-poster bed in a small ante-room off the Admirals' Room upstairs. I would willingly give up my strong desire for Jane's topaz cross to take it home. It was made by Jane, Cassandra and their mother with colourful, mainly floral remnants of material saved from the dresses they had had made, and worked in a style of quilting called 'English medallion', with panels of smaller diamond-shaped scraps round the edges, larger ones in the middle section, and a centre piece, a large diamond-shaped panel with a basket of pink flowers. The effect is endlessly pleasing and even seems rather contemporary: a Cath Kidston fantasy. In a letter written in May 1811 to Cassandra at Godmersham, Jane asks: 'Have you remembered to collect pieces for the Patchwork?' Somewhere downstairs the Austen women had sat snipping and stitching by candlelight, the floor scattered with these patches. As I admired the result, I found myself wondering who had worn which dress. Was Jane's the powder blue floral? Was Cassandra's the coral pink paisley? Had they put them on together, and admired their reflections side by side in their shared room?

Out in the lovingly tended garden at Chawton Cottage there are beech hedges and balls of box, and a shrubbery with an orchard beyond. There is a large flower border, a vegetable patch, seats and bird-feeders. I sat on a bench for a while and made notes before going round the back of the house to the outbuildings.

The family's donkey carriage, with its box seat that lifts up for storage, can still be seen in the bakehouse. The Austens kept two donkeys in a field at the end of the garden to pull it, but only one was used at a time. In the wet July of 1816, when she was already ill, Jane described a trip to the neighbouring village of Farringdon in the donkey carriage with her niece: 'We were obliged to turn back before we got there, but not soon enough to avoid a Pelter all the way.' The following January Jane wrote:

'This is not a time of year for Donkey-carriages, & our Donkeys are necessarily having so long a run of luxurious idleness that I suppose we shall find they have forgotten much of their Education when we use them again.' By the time donkey carriage weather came again, however, Jane was dying in Winchester.

Although she was increasingly debilitated by her illness, Jane's creative powers were still at their height. She revised the manuscript of *Susan*, the novel later published as *Northanger Abbey*, changing the heroine's name to Catherine, and on 8 August 1815 she began writing her last novel, now called *Persuasion*, but known to its author as *The Elliotts*, completing it almost exactly a year later, on 6 August 1816. If I were forced to pick a favourite novel, I would choose this one. The course of true love famously never does run smooth, but in Jane's other novels all is resolved between her lovers in a relatively short space of time. In *Persuasion* it is eight long years before the misunderstandings between her characters are resolved. The thrill of the moment when Captain Wentworth finally hands Anne Elliott a letter declaring the constancy of his affections – 'You pierce my soul. I am half agony, half hope' – is the ultimate in delayed literary gratification and my emotion on reading it never diminishes, no matter how many times I return to it.

It is even more gratifying when you discover how hard Jane laboured to get this ending right. James Edward Austen recalls in *A Memoir of Jane Austen* that:

> ... her performance did not satisfy her. She thought it tame and flat, and was desirous of producing something better. This weighed upon her mind, the more so probably on account of the weak state of her health; so that

one night she retired to rest in very low spirits. But such depression was little in accordance with her nature, and was soon shaken off. The next morning she awoke to more cheerful views and brighter inspirations; the sense of power revived; and imaginations resumed its course. She cancelled the condemned chapter, and wrote two others, entirely different, in its stead.[14]

In March 1817 Jane wrote to her niece Fanny: 'Miss Catherine is put upon the Shelve for the present, and I do not know that she will ever come out; – but I have something ready for Publication, which may perhaps appear about a twelvemonth hence.'

Persuasion did appear, but not in Jane Austen's lifetime. It was published by John Murray at the very end of 1817, together with *Miss Catherine*, now entitled *Northanger Abbey*, in a four-volume set. In his 'Biographical Notice of the Author', which prefaced the two novels, Henry Austen attempted to explain the delay in their publication: 'Though in composition she was equally rapid and correct, yet an invincible distrust of her own judgement induced her to withhold her works from the public, till time and many perusals had satisfied her that the charm of recent composition was dissolved.'[15]

A few months after *Persuasion* had been completed to her satisfaction Jane began the novel published years later as *Sanditon*, but finished only 50 pages before sustained periods of writing became impossible and she was forced to put it aside. In her memoir Caroline Austen recalled her melancholy last visit to Chawton to see her aunt, whose illness had by this stage confined her to her room: 'She was in her dressing gown and was sitting quite like an invalid in an arm chair – but she got up and kindly greeted us... She was very pale, her voice was weak and low... a general appearance of debility and suffering... Our visit to the sick room was a very short one... I never saw Aunt Jane again.'[16]

After Jane's death, in July 1817, her mother and Cassandra continued to live at Chawton. Despite a long history of ailments, not to say hypochondria, Mrs Austen lived to the grand age of 87, dying at Chawton in 1827. Cassandra lived on at the cottage alone after the 63-year-old Martha Lloyd married Frank Austen the following year. She helped to run a little school in the village. A Chawton man who wrote down his recollections in 1921, at the age of almost 100, remembered her. 'Miss Cassandra Austen lived at the corner house by the Pond. She took a great interest in young girls, and taught them reading, the catechism and sewing. I remember a nice dog, his name was "Link", that she had.'[17] Cassandra died in 1845, aged 72.

As at Steventon, the church and manor house of Chawton are some distance away from the rest of the village. I walked down along the old Gosport turnpike road, now a quiet road leading to a rural dead end, where molehills puncture the fields. Jane often walked this way for the pleasure of an evening stroll, or to visit her brother Edward and his children when they were staying at the Chawton Great House. They were certainly in residence during the summer of 1813 which, despite a wet July, had according to Jane, writing to Frank on his ship somewhere in the Baltic, provided some good haymaking weather: 'Edward has got all his in, in excellent order... Good encouragement for him to come again; & I really hope he will do so another Year. – The pleasure to us of having them here is so great, that if we were not the best Creatures in the World, we should not deserve it. We go on in the most comfortable way, very frequently dining together & always meeting in some part of every day.' The following summer Edward and his family did indeed return to Chawton: 'It appeared so likely to be a wet evening that I went up to the Gt House between 3 & 4, and dawdled away an hour very comfortably tho' Edward was not very brisk. The air was clearer in the Evening & he was better. – We all five walked together into the Kitchen Garden & along the Gosport Road & they drank tea with us', wrote Jane in June 1814.

Chawton Great House is a handsome Elizabethan building with tall chimneys. It stands imposingly on a rise, a carriage drive ascending to its door. After he became a more frequent visitor to Chawton, Edward Knight began to talk over possible improvements to the house and park with his sister, who wrote: 'He talks of making a new Garden; the present is a bad one and ill situated, near Mr Papillon's; he means to have the new at the top of the Lawn behind his own house. – We like to have him proving & strengthening his attachment to the place by making it better', wrote Jane in July 1813. Sadly, Jane did not live to see the walled kitchen garden that Edward introduced.

In 1826, almost ten years after Jane's death, Edward, Jane's eldest Knight nephew, came to live permanently in the Great House with his wife and their large family of 16 children. Jane's brother Edward died in 1852; some 20 years later Godmersham was sold and the Knights decamped to Chawton for good. Edward Austen Knight's descendants lived at Chawton Great House until 1914. At one time a home for Barnardos' evacuees, it is now an independent research library and study centre, focusing on women's writing in English from 1600 to 1830.

Below the Great House nestles the church, as well as the original vicarage where the eligible Mr Papillon lived, though Jane would not recognize the present building, which dates from 1871. Some years after her death Edward Knight and his son Charles, by then Chawton's rector, continued their improvements to the estate by replacing the medieval building with a new Victorian one, though this was later destroyed by fire.

In the graveyard behind the church rest the two Cassandras, namesake mother and daughter, side by side. Their lichen-covered stones are almost identical, the inscriptions equally simple. I stood for a while and contemplated them. Someone had laid a small bunch of pinks on Mrs Austen's grave. The air was still, the sunlight in the churchyard warm and dappled. It was very different from the day Jane's sister was buried. James Edward Austen described in a letter to his sister how the wind was so strong that it almost blew the pall off the coffin: 'It also struck me as remarkably emblematic of her age & condition that the wind whisked about us with so many withered beech leaves, that the coffin was thickly strewed with them before the service closed.'[18] Thus was closed the chapter of the Austens' Chawton years.

Back in the village the cricket match had resumed following a break for tea and those lovingly buttered sandwiches. I decided to soak up a little more of Chawton's Englishness before I left. Across the road from Chawton Cottage, Cassandra's Cup tea-room, its ceiling hung with dozens of tea cups, was doing a roaring trade. I found a table and drank a pot of Lapsang Souchong. Afterwards, from a plant stall outside someone's house, I bought some Laurentia, a souvenir of Chawton soil to plant in my garden at home.

I stayed the night deep in the Hampshire countryside, about six miles from Chawton, in an old manor house that had once belonged to Henry VIII. He had made a gift of it to Anne of Cleves and then, shortly afterwards, to Katherine Howard. Now a family home, it had been lovingly restored and tastefully furnished. Portraits of the two unfortunate Tudor queens gazed down as I put down my bag, shook hands with the owner and returned the enthusiastic welcome of her three glossy black Labradors. My room looked out on a little church across the road, almost hidden by a magnificent yew tree, said to be well over 2,000 years old. It was a glorious golden evening, the wooded landscape aflame in the setting sun. A hot-air balloon drifted over the hill and landed precipitously in a nearby field. A few moments later a jeep and trailer sped past in hot pursuit.

The poet Edward Thomas lived just up the road from here. At Christmas 1914, just before going off to die in the trenches of France he wrote a poem about this place called 'The Manor Farm'. It evokes perfectly the peace that, miraculously, still pervades this corner of England. The only sound he hears comes from a single fly that three cart-horses in a field are attempting to swat away with their tails. A few weeks later in January 1915, Thomas wrote his best-known poem 'Adlestrop', about a Gloucestershire village, which by a curious coincidence, was also known to Jane Austen. She visited Adlestrop with her mother and Cassandra after leaving Bath in 1806, staying with their cousin, Thomas Leigh who was rector there. In his lovely poem, Edward Thomas describes the moment after a train has stopped at the village station, a brief interlude of quiet when the sound of birdsong can take over once more, before the train continues on its journey.

I read 'The Manor Farm' as I sat downstairs later that evening with a dog's nose on my knee and a glass of wine in my hand. The poem made me think again about my visit to Chawton. To see the place where Jane Austen had lived so contentedly and produced three of her world-famous novels had been fascinating. I had taken pleasure in treading the same floorboards and pavements, and seeing with my own eyes some of the objects mentioned in her letters: the china dinner service, the patchwork, the topaz crosses. I could find no fault with the absorbing displays or the lovingly devised rooms. Yet Jane herself had been curiously absent. Her presence had somehow evaporated with the careful orchestration of her heritage and Chawton itself, though beguiling, was nothing like the place she had known, despite the fact that the fabric of the place remains essentially unaltered. Its social hierarchy has changed out of all recognition, with well-heeled commuters now living comfortably in dwellings that once housed farmworkers and the local blacksmith. The fabric of the village as Jane knew it, with its three or four families, the 'very thing' in fact to be worked on, has long since vanished beneath well-tended lawns, street lamps and tarmacked roads.

It rained heavily during the night, and the following morning the potholes in the road were full of brown water. I stepped outside, looked around at the rutted lane and the mud, the ancient church, and the graveyard with its listing grey tombstones, and noticed the scent of wet grass on the wind. There were no cars, and hardly a sound could be heard. I took another lungful of damp air. Just for a fleeting moment, in another corner of Hampshire, I felt that at last I stood in that most elusive of Shangri-Las – the England of Jane Austen.

Chapter Six
London and Surrey: 'Dissipation and vice'

I liked my solitary elegance very much, & was ready to laugh all the time at my being where I was. – I could not but feel that I had naturally small right to be parading about London in a Barouche. – Letter to her sister Cassandra, 24 May 1813

Jane Austen enjoyed London and in later life, once she was settled at Chawton, she made frequent visits to the capital. She liked spending time with Henry, who lived there – he seems to have been her favourite brother – and from 1811 onwards, the period when her novels were finally starting to be published, she often had business matters to attend to with her publishers. She certainly made the most of every visit, with nights at the theatre and shopping trips in the West End, just as visitors to London do today.

Being a visitor to London was a new and peculiar sensation for me, and I wasn't sure that I liked it. I had only recently moved to the country after living in the capital for almost 20 years. I was embracing my new out-of-town life: the children had settled in at their new school, our neighbours were welcoming and the spaciousness of our new house was liberating. If you'd told me that I had to move back to the city, I would have been distraught. Even so, as I walked down Regent Street I was having difficulty adjusting to the idea that I could no longer just get on the Tube and go home. There was something about being a Londoner that I was loath to shake off.

It also felt good to be back in Piccadilly, a part of London I've loved ever since I worked in an office there ten years ago. It had been thrilling spending every working day in the heart of tourist London, retail London, theatrical London, yet only a few steps away from the lush grass and colourful flowerbeds of Green Park. I'd drunk coffee in the local cafés and white wine in the pubs, and once a friend and I had even spent money we could ill afford on Bellinis at the Ritz. I'd bought CDs at Tower Records, books at Hatchard's, and Christmas presents at Fortnum & Mason's, and I'd window-shopped in Burlington Arcade. I'd been to exhibitions at the Royal Academy too. At the end of each working day I'd squeezed myself onto the hideously congested Victoria Line train at Green Park Underground Station and headed home, south of the river.

It was probably in Piccadilly that Jane Austen disembarked from the Hampshire coach. According to Constance Hill, in *Jane Austen: Her Homes and Her Friends*, coaches set their passengers down at The White Horse Cellar[1] close to what is now Burlington Arcade and Burlington House, which in Jane's lifetime was the private home of members of the very grand Cavendish family. Since 1867 it has been the headquarters of the Royal Academy.

After her novels had been published and she was starting to make a name for herself, Jane wrote to Cassandra that she was surely soon to find her portrait in the Academy (then based in Somerset House on the Strand): 'all white and red with my head on one side'. Many people have lamented the absence of such a portrait, instead of that rather unsatisfactory pencil sketch done by Cassandra, which is the only likeness we have of her face. In her biography of Jane Austen, published in 2001, the late Canadian novelist Carol Shields speculates as to why some of us are so fixated on what Jane Austen looked like and wonders if it is because, at the time, 'exceptional beauty occasionally gave advantage to women of little means... Austen did not marry and it must be wondered what extent her looks, handsome or unhandsome, played in that destiny.'[2] For me it's more a case of wanting to look her in the eye, in the hope of finding some clue to her genius.

Round the corner from Piccadilly I paused in Old Bond Street to eye up the flagship stores of such chic designers as Dolce & Gabbana, Chanel, and Gucci. Through the gleaming plate-glass windows I could see glamorous, pencil-thin shop assistants standing sentry: customers were conspicuously absent. In *Sense and Sensibility* it is from lodgings in Bond Street that Willoughby writes his cruel letter to Marianne, in which he professes himself quite unaware of any intimacy between them: 'My Dear Madam... If I have been so unfortunate as to give rise to a belief of more than I felt, or meant to express, I shall reproach myself for not having been more guarded in my professions of that esteem.'

The first letter we have from Jane Austen herself in London is dated 23 August 1796. She was staying in Cork Street, en route for Rowling in Kent, the home of her brother Edward before he moved to Godmersham Park: 'Here I am once more in this Scene of Dissipation & vice, and I begin already to find my

Morals corrupted.' It is a short, hurried letter: 'God Bless You – I must leave off, for we are going out', she concludes. She mentions their plan of visiting Astley's that evening. Astley's Amphitheatre, close to Westminster Bridge, was an equestrian circus opened by Philip Astley in 1770.

I walked past the fine art galleries that dominate Cork Street today and turned down Savile Row. Number 14, on the left-hand side, has a pair of white obelisks either side of the entrance steps and a plaque on the wall to commemorate the playwright Richard Brinsley Sheridan, with whose plays and productions Jane Austen was very familiar. In more recent times it has been home to the London flagship store of Hardy Amies, dressmaker to the Queen, who opened his first boutique here in 1946. The building's august period associations were offset by a widescreen television, positioned in the entrance lobby, which flashed images of the latest fashion collection at passers-by.

Further down this most sartorial of streets is Gieves & Hawkes, which was awarded its first royal warrant by King George III in 1806. Thomas Hawkes was made velvet capmaker by appointment to the king and queen, and also counted the Prince Regent as a customer. When the prince sent a message to Hawkes requesting his immediate attendance one Sunday, Hawkes, clearly a more devout man than his royal customer, sent a message back saying: 'tell his Royal Highness that for six days I serve my King, on the seventh day I serve my God'.

I turned down Sackville Street, where today there are fewer shops than in Jane Austen's time. At no. 41 was Gray's, a jeweller's shop. After Marianne has received the cruel letter from Willoughby she is overwhelmed by grief and shuts herself up in her room in the house in Portman Square that is the London home of the Dashwood sisters' hostess, Mrs Jennings. After some weeks of emotional pining she consents to go out for half an hour with her sister Elinor and Mrs Jennings, to Gray's, where Elinor is 'carrying on a negociation [*sic*] for the exchange of some old-fashioned jewels of her mother'. Gray's, however, is heaving with customers: 'All that could be done was, to sit down at that end of the counter which seemed to promise the quickest succession; one gentleman only was standing there, and it is probable that Elinor was not without hope of exciting his politeness to a quicker dispatch.' The gentleman, who turns out to be none other than dandyish Robert Ferrars, spends a quarter of an hour 'examining and debating... over every toothpick-case in the shop'. We are told that Elinor, who has never met the brother of her sweetheart Edward and so does not recognize him, is left with the 'remembrance of a person and face of strong, natural, sterling insignificance, though adorned in the first style of fashion'. No one knows better than Jane Austen how to damn with faint praise.

I threaded my way through the crowds of tourists back along Piccadilly. Back down the road towards Hyde Park Corner is the former site of the Liverpool Museum, at no. 22. Jane visited this museum of natural history in April 1811, though she was more interested in the human beings on display than in the other animals: 'my preference for Men & Woman always inclines me to attend more to the company than the sight'.

I crossed Piccadilly Circus and Leicester Square, and stopped in Cranbourn Street, sandwiched between the twin pleasure domes of the Hippodrome and the Empire Cinema. While she was staying with her brother Henry Austen in Covent Garden in March 1814, Jane wrote to Cassandra that there were 'A great many pretty Caps in the Windows of Cranbourn Alley! – I hope when you come we shall both be tempted.' At that time Leicester Square and the surrounding streets offered a good selection of shops, which had the advantage of being cheaper than those in the more fashionable parts of the West End. On an earlier visit to London, in September 1813, Jane noted that her niece Fanny bought 'her Irish' (linen) at Newton's in Leicester Square. Today drapers and hat shops have given way to a very different selection of earthly delights. Cranbourn Street offers the Crystal Rooms amusement arcade, a large branch of Burger King, and souvenir stalls selling giant Union Jacks and football shirts.

I turned down nearby Bear Street, passing six City of Westminster street sweepers all in green, engaging in a bit of lunchtime banter outside the Lovecraft Sex Shop. Then I crossed Charing Cross Road and walked down the side of Wyndham's Theatre to St Martin's Lane. Following a tip-off in Anne-Marie Edwards' book *In the Steps of Jane Austen*[3], I ducked into Goodwin's Court, which looks at first sight like the entrance to a narrow and possibly insalubrious alley. It opens up miraculously into a street of houses with carriage lamps and elegant bowed windows, a little piece of Jane Austen's London sequestered away from the fleshpots of the 21st-century West End.

Emerging from Goodwin's Court into Bedfordbury, I paused and took a look back, still enchanted by what I had seen. 'Are you lost, darlin'?' a passer-by enquired. I shook my head, and realised how odd I must look, dawdling around Central London, scribbling in a notebook and looking up at my surroundings. I had never done this when I lived in London: I'd have been in too much of a hurry, invariably late for a meeting or supper with friends.

Nearby, close to Covent Garden Market, is Henrietta Street. At no. 10 Jane Austen stayed with her brother Henry on several occasions in 1813 and 1814. Today the ground floor of the stuccoed four-storey house is home to a branch of Rohan, an outdoor clothing retailer. There is no hint of the 18th century in the shop, which has the clean lines and wooden floors of 21st-century retail. A red front door leads to the upper floors, which are now the offices of More 2; a company that offers 'integrated marketing solutions'.

The earliest surviving letter that Jane wrote from Henrietta Street is dated 15–16 September 1813, and was sent to Cassandra at Chawton. Henry's wife, Eliza, had died the previous April and shortly after her death her widower had moved from their house in Sloane Street into rooms above the Henrietta Street premises of the bank in which he was a partner. It is a delightfully gossipy letter. After a good journey from Chawton, Jane and her three oldest Kent nieces, Fanny, Elizabeth and Marianne, had enjoyed 'a most comfortable dinner of Soup, Fish, Bouillee, Partridges & an apple Tart', all prepared by Madame Bigeon, Henry's cook. At seven o'clock they had gone out again, to the Lyceum Theatre in nearby Wellington Street. Her nieces had 'revelled' in the performance of *Don Juan*, whom they 'left in Hell at ½ past 11', and they had returned to 'Soup & wine & water, & then went to our Holes', Fanny and Eliza sharing 'poor Eliza's bed'.

Jane appears to have been in high spirits, and no wonder. At 37, usually a gloomy age for a spinster of slender means, things were going well for her. The first printing of *Sense and*

Sensibility, published in 1811, had sold out, and *Pride and Prejudice* had recently been published to great acclaim. She had finished writing *Mansfield Park* that summer and *Emma* was already taking shape in her mind. Although her two published novels had appeared anonymously, word was getting around as to the identity of the author thanks to her proud brothers. You can sense that, in a quiet way, she was basking in her modest fame and fortune.

Jane's three days in London, before she travelled on to Godmersham, were hectic, with shopping, tea parties and the theatre every night. Edward made her a gift of five pounds. She took her nieces to the dentist, a visit that cost them 'many tears' and some 'screaming'. Lizzy's teeth were in a particularly bad state: 'There is a very sad hole between two of her front Teeth', her aunt reported. Jane was dubious about the dentist: 'I would not have had him look at mine for a shilling a tooth & double it.' Later the same day Jane had her hair done by a Mr Hall, who 'curled her out at a great rate'. Jane thought that the result looked 'hideous' and longed for a 'snug cap instead', but 'my companions silenced me by their admiration'.

Directly opposite no. 10 Henrietta Street is an alley that leads to the delightful garden and forecourt of St Paul's, Covent Garden, otherwise known as the Actors' Church. The paths are lined with benches, each given in memory of a different actor. I plonked myself down on 'Carmen Silvera, Actress 1922–2002' and averted my eyes from the snogging couple opposite. The church was designed by Inigo Jones and completed in 1633. The first known victim of the Great Plague of 1665, Margaret

Porteous, was buried in the churchyard on 12 April. In his diary entry for 9 May 1662 Samuel Pepys mentions an 'Italian puppet play' performed under the church portico. This was the first recorded Punch and Judy show, an event commemorated by an annual service at St Paul's each May.

The connection between St Paul's Church and the theatre world dates from the establishment of the Theatre Royal in nearby Drury Lane, in 1663, and was later strengthened by the opening of the Covent Garden Theatre, now the Royal Opera House, in 1723. The church now contains a veritable cast list of memorial tablets to the great and good of the British stage and screen. The opening scene of Shaw's *Pygmalion* takes place here, as the stage directions indicate: 'London at 11.15 p.m. Torrents of heavy summer rain. Cab whistles blowing frantically in all directions. Pedestrians running for shelter in the portico of St Paul's Church.' Freddy, who is trying desperately to secure a cab for his sheltering mother and sister, collides with a flower girl, scattering her basket. 'Theres manners f' yer! Too banches o voylets trod in the mad', says Eliza Doolittle, for it is she.

Today St Paul's Church provides a retreat from Covent Garden and its crowds of tourists. I sat inside, enclosed by one of the high wooden pews, the quiet only occasionally broken by the whoops of the crowd gathered round the busker outside.

I feel sure that Jane Austen must have come here, even though no evidence that she did so has survived: it's a historic and beautiful church, after all, and it's just a step away from Henry's house. Perhaps she even sat in the same pew and listened to the Reverend Edward Embry, whose ministry at St Paul's is commemorated by a grave memorial, typical of the 19th century, that tells how he 'departed this life on 24th February 1817, aged

72', after being '30 years curate and 7 years rector of this parish', had been 'solemnly impressed with the awful responsibility attached to the pastoral office', and had 'watched over his flock as one who knew he must render an account'.

Jane was back in Henrietta Street in March 1814 for a stay of almost three weeks. She travelled up by carriage with Henry from Chawton. On the way they read through the proofs of *Mansfield Park*, which was published a couple of months later. 'Henry's approbation hitherto is even equal to my wishes', Jane wrote to Cassandra from a 'new Table' in the front room: 'he says it is very different from the other two, but does not appear to think it at all inferior.' Jane was very tired after her journey, but had recovered by the following day: 'I slept to a miracle & am lovely today.' There were heavy snowfalls in London, but also the exciting prospect of a trip to Drury Lane Theatre that coming Saturday night to see Edmund Kean in The Merchant of Venice: 'So great is the rage for seeing Keen [sic]' that 'only a 3rd or 4th row could be got'.

I took the Tube from Covent Garden to Knightsbridge. Later in 1814 Henry Austen left Henrietta Street and took a house at 23 Hans Place, now a stone's throw from Harrods. Henry already knew the area well: Hans Place is just round the corner from the Sloane Street house where Henry had previously lived with Eliza. Jane had stayed with them there in 1811 and 1813. In the early 19th century much of this area was still fields and it was only just beginning to be developed as a residential district. Jane writes at one point of 'walking into town to do her shopping'. London was a fraction of the size that it is today; its western limits marked by Park Lane and Edgware Road. Parts of what is now inner London, such as Islington and Hackney, Paddington and Kensington, were still villages.

As I walked down the chic and urbane Sloane Street of today, I found it virtually impossible to transport my mind back to such a time. Tall buildings line each side of the road and behind them stand dense rows of Victorian mansion blocks. Prosperity oozes from every door. It's another place of designer boutiques – Marni, Gucci, Dior, Chanel – private dentists charging much more than 'a shilling a tooth and double it', posh little prep schools and foreign embassies. A gardener at the Danish Embassy was manicuring the box hedges outside. Small girls just out of school jigged along in tartan skirts and navy cardigans.

The house at no. 64 Sloane Street where Henry and Eliza lived no longer exists. It has been replaced by a seven-storey building in Art Nouveau style, with three curious round windows on the sixth floor. When Jane Austen stayed here she spent a good deal of her time shopping. She wrote to Cassandra in April 1811: 'I am sorry to tell you that I am getting very extravagant & spending all my Money; & what is worse for you, I have been spending yours too.' Every trip to London provided an opportunity to catch up with the latest fashions ('I find the Muslin is not so wide as it used to be') and to fulfil errands for those left behind, eager for some treats from the big city. Her letters from London record the purchase of many different items, including checked muslin, bugle trimming and silk stockings. She was careful to record the cost of everything and often appealed to Cassandra to reassure her that she had not been imprudent.

A country spinster she may have been, but Jane Austen was not uninterested in her appearance, although she often employs self-deprecating humour on the subject: 'Now nothing can satisfy me but I must have a straw hat, of the riding hat shape. I am really very shocking; but it will not be dear at a Guinea', she wrote to Cassandra in April 1811. When during this same visit someone at a party made an approving remark about her 35-year-old appearance, she wrote '"A pleasing looking young woman"; that must do... one cannot pretend to anything better now – thankful to have it continued a few years longer!'

The delights of London were not confined to shopping and theatre-going, however. From Sloane Street Jane and Henry visited an exhibition held in Spring Gardens by the Society of Painters in Oil and Water Colours. Jane found a small portrait 'excessively like' Mrs Bingley of *Pride and Prejudice*. 'I went in hopes of seeing one of her Sister, but there was no Mrs Darcy', she wrote in May 1813. She went in search of Mrs Darcy again at an exhibition at Somerset House, but in vain: 'I can only imagine that Mr D prizes any Picture of her too much to like it should be exposed to public eye.' She was clearly enjoying herself immensely: 'I had great amusement among the Pictures; & the Driving about, the Carriage been [*sic*] open, was very pleasant.' She had taken to being driven around on her own in Henry's barouche, a liberating novelty for a single woman who would normally have been chaperoned.

In Hans Place more red-brick mansion blocks crowd round a private central garden, ringed with parking meters and expensive cars. Number 23, formerly Henry Austen's house, is now the end of a lofty Victorian block, each house almost indistinguishable from the one next door, except for no. 30, the sole remaining 18th-century house in the row, its elegant lines sandwiched uncomfortably between its much taller and uglier neighbours.

Henry's house probably looked very similar. 'It is a delightful Place', Jane reported to Cassandra on her first visit, in August 1814. 'I find more space & comfort in the rooms than I had supposed, & the Garden is quite a Love.' Shortly afterwards her brothers James and Edward arrived in town: 'Their business is about Teeth and Wigs', Jane wrote. After a little over a year as a widower Henry was starting to entertain the idea of remarrying and introduced a couple of his 'favourites' to Jane, hopeful of her approval. Jane stayed for 12 days, during which there were 'two or three very little dinner-parties at home, some delightful Drives in the Curricle and quiet tea-drinkings with the Tilsons' (James Tilson was Henry's partner in the Henrietta Street bank). As usual, she recorded the latest fashions, this time for Martha Lloyd, who was staying in Bath: 'I am amused by the present style of female dress; – the coloured petticoats with braces over the white Spencers & enormous Bonnets upon the full stretch, are quite entertaining.'

I peered into the private garden in the centre of Hans Place. It was jungly and appealing, but the gate was firmly padlocked, and a notice sternly listed the Rules and Regulations: 'No Dogs. No Games Whatever. No Servants are Permitted in the Garden Unless in Charge of Children of Subscribers.' Close by stood a marble drinking fountain, grubby and full of stagnant water. It commemorates Herbert Stewart and his son Geoffrey, a Coldstream Guard, killed, aged 36, in action in France in 1914.

I looked around. With Harrods as the local corner shop, Hans Place is serious real estate. There were skips and scaffolding everywhere, signs that property developers were at large. On a nearby balcony a cleaning lady in yellow Marigolds was washing the windows.

At the end of November 1814 Jane was back at Hans Place again and this time she had business with her publisher, Thomas Egerton. Jane was hopeful that Egerton would agree to bring out a second edition of *Mansfield Park*, despite the fact that it had not sold as well as either *Sense and Sensibility* or *Pride and Prejudice*. Jane wrote to her niece Fanny Knight: 'People are more ready to borrow & praise, than to buy – which I cannot wonder at, but tho' I like praise as well as anybody, I like what Edward calls Pewter too.' Unfortunately for Jane and her bank balance, Egerton refused.

Jane's last and probably longest stay in London was in November and December 1815. There was little time for shopping, walking in the park or driving about in carriages. Since Egerton's refusal the previous autumn, Henry had been busy on his sister's behalf and, thanks to his efforts, Jane had acquired a new publisher, John Murray of Albermarle Street, who had agreed to publish a second edition of *Mansfield Park*, as well as Jane's fourth novel, *Emma*.

Henry had done well. John Murray was probably the most celebrated and influential publisher of the day. His authors included Sir Walter Scott, George Crabbe and, most notoriously, Lord Byron, who became his close friend and correspondent. Three years before, in 1812, Murray had published Byron's second book, *Childe Harold's Pilgrimage*. It sold out in five days, leading Byron to remark: 'I awoke one morning and found myself famous.' After

Byron's death in 1824 Murray burned the poet's memoirs in the fireplace in his office in order to protect his reputation.

Jane Austen was certainly familiar with Byron's work. In *Persuasion* Anne Elliot and Captain Benwick, staying at Lyme Regis, discuss the relative merits of Byron's poems 'Giaour' and 'The Bride of Abydos'. The recently bereaved Benwick shows himself to be so 'intimately acquainted' with all Byron's 'impassioned descriptions of hopeless agony' that Anne feels compelled to recommend some calmer reading.

The most prominent publisher of the day he may have been, but John Murray still tried to pull a fast one on the lady author from Hampshire. In October 1815 Jane told Cassandra: 'Mr Murray's Letter is come; he is a Rogue of course, but a civil one.' Murray had offered Jane £450 to publish *Emma*, but wanted the copyrights of *Mansfield Park* and *Sense and Sensibility* thrown in. Jane was roused and charmed at the same time: 'It will end in my publishing for myself I dare say. He sends more praise however than I expected. It is an amusing Letter.'

Then Henry became ill with a bilious fever. An apothecary was called, a Mr Haydon from the corner of Sloane Street, who took 20 ounces of blood from his patient each day. Jane dispensed 'Medicine, Tea and Barley Water'. Henry managed to dictate a reply to John Murray, refusing the publisher's offer on behalf of his sister: 'The Terms you offer are so very inferior to what we had expected, that I am apprehensive of having made some great Error in my Arithmetical Calculation.'

Henry's continued illness eventually forced Jane to tackle John Murray herself. She wrote to him in early November, 'desirous of coming to some decision on the affair in question' and asking him to call at Hans Place. She eventually settled for publication on commission, with Murray to keep 10 per cent of the profits.

One of the doctors called in to attend on Henry, a Dr Baillie, was also a physician at court. He told Jane that the Prince Regent was an admirer of her work. Jane was certainly no admirer of the prince. Of his estranged wife, Princess Caroline, she had once written (in February 1813): 'I shall support her as long as I can because she is a Woman, and because I hate her Husband.' Nevertheless, when the Prince's librarian, James Stanier Clarke, called on Jane and invited her to visit the library at Carlton House, the Regent's luxurious London house in St James's, she went. Then Stanier hinted that she might like to dedicate her next book to the prince. This was tantamount to a royal command and accordingly *Emma* was dedicated to him, presumably with mixed feelings on the part of 'His Royal Highness's Dutiful, and Obedient Humble Servant, The Author'. John Murray printed 2,000 copies of *Emma*, the largest edition of any of her works to date, and charged 21 shillings for the three volumes.

By the time *Emma* was published, in early 1816, Henry had recovered and Jane was back at Chawton. As far as we know, she never visited London again. A few months later Henry's bank failed and he went bankrupt. Henry decided that he had had enough of the financial world and of the city. Soon afterwards he took holy orders and returned to Chawton, giving up the house in Hans Place.

Up on Box Hill a rugby ball was being chucked across the car park as vehicle after vehicle crunched across the gravel, parked, and disgorged balls, buggies and coolbags. It was a Bank

Holiday Monday, and a constant stream of cars was zigzagging its way up the chalk ridge in search of fresh air and fun. The picnic tables around the National Trust Visitor Centre were already full. Bare arms and legs were enjoying their first proper airing of the year, and there was a pervasive smell of cigarette smoke. A group of cyclists in matching Lycra outfits clutched cups of coffee and compared inclines.

People have been coming to Box Hill in search of recreation for centuries. In *A Tour through the Whole Island of Great Britain* (1724–6) Daniel Defoe observed that 'here every Sunday, during the summer season, there used to be a rendez-vous of coaches and horsemen, with abundance of gentleman and ladies from Epsome to take the air, and walk in the box-woods; and in a word, divert, or debauch, or perhaps both, as they thought fit'.[4]

I'd been to Box Hill only once before, years ago, as a naïve volunteer youth worker on a summer holiday project, helping to look after a group of challenging teenagers from a South London sink estate. I was barely older than they were and, as a nice middle-class girl from the provinces, I was completely clueless about how to talk to them. I spent almost no time admiring the scenery and a lot of time trying to stop them absconding to investigate the delights of nearby Dorking.

Box Hill is a lazy, southern kind of hill. You don't have to work for the views; you can drive to the top and totter the few steps from the car park to the main viewpoint. Buggies, toddling children and high heels are all quite feasible accoutrements. Box Hill could never be called wild and undiscovered, what with its tarmacked road and speed bumps, and the railway running just below. Yet the rolling downland scenery is beautiful, in a very English kind of way, and still provides a habitat for a remarkable variety of flora and fauna, as well as the ancient box woodland that gives the escarpment its name.

Box Hill is, of course, the scene of the fateful picnic in *Emma*, when Emma is rude to Miss Bates, much to the chagrin of Mr Knightley. It is only when Emma has lost his good opinion that it dawns on her how much she cares for him. The outing is somewhat ill-starred from the beginning. Emma, seeking as ever to avoid the vulgar Mrs Elton and her *caro sposo*, hopes that it will be done in a 'quiet, unpretending, elegant way, infinitely superior to the bustle and preparation, the regular eating and drinking, and pic-nic parade of the Eltons and Sucklings'. Mr Weston, however, invites all and sundry, maintaining that 'One cannot have too large a party. A large party secures its own amusement.'

On the day of the excursion the weather is fine, and 'all other outward circumstances of arrangement, accommodation and punctuality were in favour of a pleasant party'. Despite a 'burst of admiration' on first arriving, however, there is something lacking: 'There was a languor, a want of spirits, a want of union, which could not be got over.' To fill the void Emma flirts outrageously with Frank Churchill, who responds enthusiastically and loudly: 'Let every body on the Hill hear me if they can. Let my accents swell to Mickleham on one side, and Dorking on the other.' In an attempt to rouse the other members of the party Frank proposes a game in which each person must say 'one thing very clever... two things moderately clever... or three things very dull indeed'. When Miss Bates opts for three things Emma cannot help herself: 'Ah! ma'am, but there may be a difficulty. Pardon me, but you will be limited as to number – only three at once.'

Jane Austen's novels contain very few topographical descriptions, and *Emma* is no exception. Even the spectacular view from

Box Hill is hardly alluded to. The setting is merely the backdrop to a pivotal chapter of the novel in which all Emma's plans and pretensions start to unravel, and she begins to understand her true feelings and to pay proper attention to those of others. Claire Tomalin makes a perceptive comment about *Emma* in her biography of Jane: 'I sometimes think Austen may have had her first flash of an idea for *Emma* as she wrote Fanny's words to Henry Crawford: "We have all a better guide in ourselves, if we would attend to it, than any other person can be."'[5] Fanny Price, the hardest of all Jane's heroines to warm to at first, gets it right again.

Despite Jane Austen's apparent lack of interest in the scenery, readers inspired by *Emma* to come to Box Hill are unlikely to be disappointed. The view south is enchanting, soothingly pastoral and English to the very last twig. Cows graze in the fields below as their calves canter around playfully. The covers stand at the ready on a nearby cricket field. Handsome mansions peep out over the treetops, and the grass is studded with primroses and forget-me-nots.

Box Hill is the ideal outing for those who live in the city. It suits both those desperate for a dose of real countryside, and those who are suspicious of it and unwilling to venture far from 'civilization'. There are reassuring signs of the 21st century everywhere, from the planes hanging low over Gatwick Airport on the horizon to the long scar of the railway line heading south. People sit on benches, rustling crisp packets. Children roll down the hill as Catherine Morland did, gathering grass as they go. Above, grey clouds glower in true Bank Holiday tradition.

Of course, you can always go shopping, as a helpful National Trust sign points out: 'Box Hill is of international importance for its chalk grassland and woodland, including the Box trees from which it gets its name. Plus all this natural interest is only a short stroll away from the shop.' The shop, I discovered, was the 'very first to be dressed in the brand new countryside concept'. Lavender eye-masks, bath cubes and drawer liners were laid out enticingly in the hope of fetching up in a day tripper's bathroom cupboard somewhere. Tucked away in a corner was a much more seductive display of touchy-feely objects dug up on the Hill: a deer skull and some lovely fossils.

It is possible to get away from the crowds and sit, as Emma longs to after tiring of the company at the picnic, 'almost alone, and quite unattended to, in tranquil observation of the beautiful views beneath her'. Ambling along one of the many footpaths I came across the memorial stone to Major Peter Labellière, an officer in the Royal Marines who died in Jane Austen's lifetime, aged 75: 'An eccentric resident of Dorking was buried here head downwards, 11th July 1800.' Having accurately predicted the date of his death, Major Labellière left two most particular wishes in his will: first, that the youngest son and daughter of his landlady should be invited to dance on his coffin and, second, that he should be buried upside down on Box Hill. Since the world was completely topsy-turvey, he reasoned, he was sure to be the right way up in the end.

Jane Austen herself may well have come to Box Hill: it would help to explain her choice of such a specific setting for the crucial picnic scene. She is certainly known to have stayed at the vicarage in nearby Great Bookham. Her mother's first cousin, also called Cassandra, was married to the incumbent, the Reverend Samuel Cooke, who was also Jane's godfather. Cooke was vicar at Great Bookham for more than 50 years, from 1769 until his death in 1820. Jane was not always keen to stay with the Cookes and in a letter of January 1799 she remarks to Cassandra: 'I can assure You that I dread the idea of going to Bookham as much as you can do.' Jane's godfather, however, was an admirer of her work, particularly *Mansfield Park*. According to another of Jane's letters, he proclaimed it 'the most sensible Novel he ever read, and the manner in which I treat the Clergy, delights them very much'.

Plenty of other writers have been familiar with Box Hill. The novelist and poet George Meredith lived at the bottom of the hill in a flint and brick house where he was visited by such literary luminaries of the time as J.M. Barrie, George Gissing, Henry James and Robert Louis Stevenson. The novelist Fanny Burney lived in Great Bookham between 1793 and 1797, with her husband General d'Arblay, a French aristocrat in exile. The d'Arblays met the Cookes on many occasions, but it is not known if they ever met Jane. That Jane admired and learned from Fanny Burney's work is undeniable. One of my favourite of all Jane's descriptions of people in her letters concerns an acquaintance she met in Kent in September 1796: 'Miss Fletcher and I were very thick, but I am the thinnest of the two – She wore her purple Muslin, which is pretty enough tho' it does not become her complexion. There are two Traits in her Character which are pleasing; namely, she admires Camilla [a novel by Burney], & drinks no cream in her Tea.' It is believed that Jane took the title *Pride and Prejudice* from the end of another of Burney's novels, *Cecilia*.

Emma is the only one of Jane Austen's novels I studied at school. To my embarrassment, our recent house move had uncovered some of my practice A-Level essays, including one I wrote about

Emma in January 1982. In a curly, girly hand, very unlike the spiky writing I have today, I wrote my answer to the question: '"There is nothing more in *Emma* than a pleasing look at country life." Discuss this statement.' Though I later did well in the actual exam, the essay is poor. I do a lot of beating about the bush, fail to come to many salient points and wouldn't swear to not having copied certain phrases from some study guide or other. 'This promises much but doesn't produce all', my teacher concluded. 'At times you verge on the journalistic.' The one thing I did get right was my assessment of Emma's fateful remark to Miss Bates as 'a perfect example of Jane Austen's wicked humour, which is often not at all charming!' Now that I'm older and a good deal more cynical, it is Jane's wicked remarks, both in her letters and in her novels, that give me the most pleasure, despite twinges of sympathy for Miss Bates and the muslin-clad Miss Fletcher.

Cars continued to roar past us up the road as I left Box Hill. I passed through Great Bookham, now prime commuter territory, on the way back to Godalming, where I was staying. The sun was shining and gardeners were waging war on dandelions. It was time for a cup of tea, to be drunk, in tribute to Miss Fletcher, without cream.

Chapter Seven
Winchester: 'July in showers'

Where once we are buried you think we are dead
But behold me Immortal! – From an untitled poem
dated 15 July 1817[1]

I felt weary as I set out for Winchester. Normally the three-hour train journey wouldn't have bothered me in the least. I loved having time and space to read and think, and I was well-supplied with books, home-made biscuits, grapes and decent coffee, but while I was waiting at Reading for a delayed connection the commuter hustle of the station started to get to me and I longed to be back at home. Maybe it was the idea of coming to the end of the road, tracing Jane Austen's final journey that was starting to depress me.

At least Reading was an appropriate place to be stuck. Jane Austen came here in 1785, at the age of nine, to attend the Abbey School with Cassandra. Her father hadn't intended to send Jane at all, but she had refused to be separated from her sister. Their mother remarked years later: 'If Cassandra's head had been going to be cut off, Jane would have her's [*sic*] cut off too.'[2] The school was run by a Mrs La Tournelle, who had, as Claire Tomalin puts it in her biography of Jane, 'a cork leg of mysterious origin'.[3] The curriculum does not appear to have been very exacting and Tomalin concludes that it was 'a harmless, slatternly place'. This was Jane's only period away from the bosom of her family and it didn't last long: after one year there the girls left Reading and returned home to Steventon, their boarding-school adventure over.

Thirty years later the first signs of what was to be Jane Austen's final illness appeared, though you would not know it from the unfailingly cheerful letters she sent from Chawton throughout 1816. It was still a productive time : she was engrossed in writing *The Elliots*, her working title for *Persuasion*, and revising the manuscript of *Susan*, now known as *Northanger Abbey*. On the domestic front there was rarely a dull moment, as Chawton Cottage was alive with the comings and goings of Jane's many nieces and nephews. She had also added the role of great-aunt to her repertoire after the birth of Anna Jemima, daughter of her niece, late the previous summer.

However, something wasn't right. In May Jane and Cassandra set off to take the waters at Cheltenham, in the hope of alleviating the symptoms of Jane's illness. We don't know if she derived any benefit from her stay there, but she was soon back in Chawton. In July she finished *Persuasion* and put the manuscript aside.

It was in September that she began to hint in her letters that all was not well. She wrote to Cassandra, who had returned to Cheltenham with Mary, the wife of their brother James: 'Thank you, my Back has given me scarcely any pain for many days. I am nursing myself up now into as beautiful a state as I can.'

In December, however, Jane disclosed in a letter to her nephew James Edward that she had had to decline an invitation to dine with her niece Anna at nearby Wyards Farm a mile away: 'The walk is beyond my strength (though I am otherwise very well).' In January 1817 she declared that she was 'getting stronger than I was half a year ago, & can so perfectly well walk to Alton, or back again, without that slightest fatigue that I hope to be able to do both when Summer comes'. It was a vain hope.

Jane's illness did not prevent her from starting a new novel in January 1817. It's astonishing that someone so unwell should embark on such a sharp satire of hypochondria, or feel like poking such merciless fun at illness. *Sanditon*, as we have seen, is set in a small village that is being developed into a seaside resort. Mr Parker, one of the prime movers behind the development, has two sisters, Diana and Susan, of whom he remarks 'I do not believe they know what a day's health is', and a younger brother, Arthur, who is 'so delicate he can engage in no profession'.

At first it seems that all three will be too ill to travel to Sanditon. Diana feels that the sea will probably be the 'death' of her, afflicted as she is by her 'old grievance', which has left her 'hardly able to crawl from her bed to the sofa'. Susan, meanwhile, having endured six leeches a day for ten days, to no avail, has been persuaded by her sister that the cause of her headache lies in her gums and so has had three teeth drawn. Now she can 'only speak in a whisper' – and faints away twice 'on poor Arthur's trying to suppress a cough'. Arthur himself is 'tolerably well', but 'Diana fears for his liver'. Eventually, however, the siblings make it to Sanditon, reasonably unscathed by the journey. Even Susan has no 'hysterics of consequence' until they have all but arrived. The book's heroine, the eminently sensible Charlotte Heywood, observes the visitors' strange behaviour and concludes that they have no symptoms that 'she would not have undertaken to cure, by putting out the fire, opening the window, and disposing of the drops and salts by means of one or the other'. It's clear that Jane too had little patience with illness. 'Sickness', she wrote to her niece Fanny Knight in March 1817, 'is a dangerous Indulgence at my time of Life.' She so wanted to be busy, to be making herself useful, to be writing. In *Sanditon* the delusion of ill health is something to be satirized as the consequence of having an idle mind: 'Disorders and recoveries so very much out of the common way, seemed more like the amusement of eager minds in want of employment than of actual afflictions and relief.' It's almost as if Jane believed that she could write away her own illness by making fun of those who languished on sofas. Her brother Henry later wrote that she supported 'all the varying pain, irksomeness, and tedium attendant on decaying nature… with a truly elastic cheerfulness'.[4]

Despite her best efforts, her symptoms continued to worsen. After 18 March even *Sanditon* was put aside, to remain forever unfinished. We shall sadly never know what fate Jane had in mind for her hilarious trio of *malades imaginaires*.

There was nothing imaginary about her own symptoms. In early April, after a bilious attack and fever, Jane admitted to having felt 'too unwell this last fortnight to write anything that was not absolutely necessary'. On Sunday 27 April she wrote her last will and testament, in which she left everything to Cassandra, apart from legacies of £50 each to her brother Henry and, in a compassionate gesture, his former cook, Madame Bigeon, who had lost everything when Henry's bank had collapsed the previous year.

A few days later it was agreed that Jane should travel the 16 miles from Chawton to Winchester to seek medical care. Since its foundation in 1736 the hospital at Winchester had developed an excellent reputation and Jane was to be under the direct care of one of its 'capital surgeons', Giles King Lyford, who had already treated Jane with some success. Describing herself in a letter to Anne Sharp, the former governess at Godmersham with whom she was still affectionately in touch, as 'a very genteel, portable sort of an Invalid', she set off on 24 May, accompanied by Cassandra, in their brother Edward's carriage. Their brother Henry and their nephew William rode alongside in the rain for most of the way.

Having arrived in Winchester, I walked across the city to the house where Jane spent the final weeks of her life, in College Street. The sun was shining and the city centre was busy with shoppers and children on holiday from school for Easter. However, as I turned down a lane away from the High Street towards the cathedral precincts, a blissful quiet descended and the traffic noise was reduced to a distant hum, overlaid with spring birdsong.

I walked slowly down College Street. There it was: no. 8, a slightly tatty three-storey house, built in the 18th century, with its wall plaque reading: 'In This House, Jane Austen Lived Her Last Days And Died, 18th July 1817.' The house now belongs to Winchester College, which adjoins it, and looks as if it has scarcely changed since its most famous former resident tried so good-humouredly to persuade herself and others that she was getting better, as in a letter to her nephew James Edward on 27 May: 'I will not boast of my handwriting; neither that, nor my face have yet recovered their proper beauty, but in other respects I am gaining strength.'

During the daytime she managed, now and again, to walk from room to room, but mostly she stayed on the sofa, in a cruel echo of the gloriously indolent Diana Parker in *Sanditon*. The College Street lodgings, she reported in a letter of 27 May, were very comfortable: 'We have a neat little Drawing-room with a Bow-window overlooking Dr Gabell's garden.' Gabell was then Headmaster of Winchester College and had presided over the education of Jane's Knight nephews.

I looked up at that same bow window as I sat on the front wall of the garden. Daffodils waved in the breeze and a large magnolia tree leaned against the ancient wall of the cathedral close. There were few passers-by. I tried to decide if Jane would have been able to see over the wall and across to the cathedral beyond. If so, it must have been a tantalizing view. She was able to go outdoors only once, in a sedan chair, but she hoped that when the weather improved she might be 'promoted to a wheel-chair'.

Perhaps the prospect of the summer warmth to come lifted the sisters' spirits a little and brought some hope. If so, it was cruelly short-lived, for, in the early hours of 18 July, Jane Austen died in her sister Cassandra's arms. She was 41 years old. Two days later Cassandra wrote to Fanny Knight: 'She felt herself to be dying about half an hour before she became tranquil & aparently [*sic*] unconscious. When I asked her if there was any thing she wanted, her answer was she wanted nothing but death & some of her words were "God grant me patience. Pray for me, Oh Pray for me."' Then Cassandra added: 'She was the sun of my life, the gilder of every pleasure, the soother of every sorrow.'[5]

After a while I got up from the wall and retraced my steps back through the city walls under Kingsgate, where, on a whim, I pushed open a door and climbed some steps into the little medieval church of St Swithins-by-Kingsgate, situated right above the arch of Kingsgate. It was two days before Good Friday and a notice showed that week's Gospel, a passage from St John: 'Now my soul is in turmoil, and what am I to say? Father, save me from this hour.'

Jane Austen's funeral took place in Winchester Cathedral on the following Thursday 24 July 1817. The fact that the Austens were a clerical family seems to have ensured that there was no difficulty in getting permission for Jane to be buried in such a hallowed place. A vault was made ready in the north aisle of the cathedral while Jane's body lay in an open coffin in the dining room of 8 College Street. 'Even now', Cassandra wrote, gazing upon her dead sister, 'there is such a sweet serene air over her countenance as is quite pleasant to contemplate.'

What did Jane Austen die of? She is generally thought to have been suffering from Addison's disease, though in 1817 no one had heard of such a complaint, since Addison's was named only in 1855, by Dr Thomas Addison, the pioneering endocrinologist who first described the disease (he was also one of the first doctors to provide a detailed description of appendicitis). Addison's is a rare condition, occurring in around 1 in 40,000 people. It arises when the adrenal glands do not make enough cortisol, a steroid hormone that regulates blood pressure and the immune system. Its symptoms include steadily worsening fatigue, a loss of appetite, light-headedness, nausea, irritability and depression. It also produces a darkening of the skin that, in the words of the website of the Addison's Disease Self Help Group, looks like an 'inappropriate tan on a person who feels very sick'.[6]

The general belief that Jane Austen died from Addison's disease stemmed originally from an article in the *British Medical*

Journal (July 1964) by a distinguished surgeon and expert on the history of medicine, Sir Zachary Cope. He concluded that Addison's was the cause primarily because of the changes that we know occurred in her skin colour. However, while Jane's illness did indeed induce some discolouration to her face, she seems not to have been 'tanned'. She described her 'Looks' to Fanny Knight in March 1817 as being 'black & white and every wrong colour'. Because of this discrepancy recent biographers are increasingly tending to revise the diagnosis of Addison's. Claire Tomalin, for example, suggests in an appendix to her biography of Jane that she may have died of a lymphoma such as Hodgkin's disease, a form of cancer.[7] In the early 19th century, of course, it was much more common to die in one's 40s, yet Jane Austen, the seventh of eight children, was the first among them to die. With the exception of her eldest brother James, who died in 1819 at the age of 54, the Austens were a family of long-lived individuals. Jane's mother lived to 87 and six of her siblings, including Cassandra, lived well into their 70s or 80s. Jane's last surviving brother was Admiral Frank Austen, who was 91 when he died in 1865. Having experienced perhaps the most dangerous life of all the Austen brothers and sisters, much of it at sea and in the line of fire, Frank outlived them all. Many people have suffered much crueller fates than Jane Austen's, but as I wandered around Winchester, like so many before me, I couldn't help cursing whatever quirk of genetics or environment it was that condemned her to an early grave.

Jane's funeral was arranged for an early hour on 24 July, so as not to disrupt the schedule of daily services in the cathedral. The cortege consisted of Jane's brothers, Edward, Henry and Francis, and her nephew James Edward, who rode over from Steventon.

It was not then customary for women to attend funerals, so Cassandra stayed away. Instead she 'watched the little mournful procession the length of the street & and when it turned from my sight I had lost her forever.'[8] A few days later she returned to Chawton.

I followed the route of Jane's funeral procession into the cathedral precincts and round to the west door. From a nearby house came the sound of choirboys stopping and starting over a tricky line as they rehearsed an Easter canticle. As I rounded the corner of the cathedral I almost ran into a couple of policemen with sniffer dogs. I snapped out of the 19th century in an instant and looked after them, alarmed. Had I stumbled on a crime scene?

In fact I'd come to Winchester on the day of a royal visit. I didn't actually see the Princess Royal, who had come to accept the freedom of the city on behalf of the King's Royal Hussars, of whom she is colonel in chief, but as I arrived at the cathedral a small detachment of hussars on horseback was lining up for a photo call, with the west front as a backdrop. They were causing quite a stir in their full dress uniforms, swords at the ready. Proud relatives waited nearby, comparing the photographs they'd taken on their mobile phones, while children ran around waving balloons. Kitty and Lydia Bennet of *Pride and Prejudice* would have enjoyed this scene. The arrival of the officers and men of 'the – shires' regiment, who have come to spend the winter quartered in Meryton, brings the Bennet girls into contact with a certain George Wickham. Deirdre Le Faye describes in *Jane Austen: The World of Her Novels* how the militia was periodically paraded for review by a visiting general, in a public relations exercise designed to demonstrate to the public how well they were being defended. The soldiers spent a day march-ing, drilling, firing and engaging in pretend skirmishes, much to the delight of the locals, particularly the girls. 'If you are a good girl for the next ten years', Mr Bennet says to Kitty, 'I will take you to a review at the end of them.' [9]

'It is a satisfaction to me', Cassandra wrote in her letter to Fanny Knight following Jane's death, 'that her dear remains are to lie in a Building she admird [sic] so much.' Winchester Cathedral is an impressive place for a country parson's daughter to be buried. When it was begun, in 1079, it was the largest church north of the Alps, and was intended as a symbol of Norman power and prestige. The Norman cathedral was built on the site of an earlier Saxon church, which had been a place of pilgrimage for the relics of St Swithun, a former Bishop of Winchester, for centuries.

On a rainy 15 July, three days before she died, Jane Austen wrote a comic poem about St Swithun in honour of his saint's day, an important festival in the life of the cathedral as well as a day beloved of weather forecasters. Dictating to Cassandra, she imagined the saint laying a curse on the Winchester Races, which were also taking place that day. St Swithun addresses the town's citizens who, forgetting their patron saint, have dared to hold such a secular event on his holy day ('Venta' was the Roman name for Winchester):

> Oh! subjects rebellious! Oh Venta depraved
> When once we are buried you think we are dead
> But behold me Immortal! By vice you're enslaved
> You have sinn'd & must suffer, then farther he said

These races and revels and dissolute measures
With which you're debasing a neighbouring Plain
Let them stand – You shall meet with your curse in your
    pleasures
Set off for your course, I'll pursue with my rain.
Ye cannot but know my command o'er July
Henceforward I'll triumph in shewing my powers
Shift your race as you will it shall never be dry
The curse upon Venta is July in showers.

Jane Austen's tomb is right in the middle of the north aisle of the cathedral, not far from the entrance desk. A black slab of marble marks the place, which has now become one of the most visited parts of the cathedral. 'In Memory of Jane Austen', it says: 'She departed this life on the 18th July 1817 aged 41, after a long illness, supported with the patience and hopes of a Christian.'

I sat down as a shaft of sunlight moved across the black slab, obscuring the words. Nearby a line of votive candles, by the beautiful 12th-century font of black Tournai marble, cast rippling shadows on the floor.

After a few minutes an Australian woman came by, accompanied by a red-robed member of the cathedral clergy. 'Here it is', he said. 'It says she was a lovely lady, but it doesn't mention her books, you know.' It famously doesn't, but they were not the preoccupation of Jane's age. The writer of her epitaph chose instead to celebrate 'the benevolence of her heart, the sweetness of her temper, and the extraordinary endowments of her mind', and to declare that her 'intimate connections' would be consoled by a 'firm though humble hope that her charity, devotion, faith and purity have rendered her soul acceptable in the sight of her REDEEMER'.

In 1872 a brass plaque was added to the wall above the tomb with a note about her novels and in 1900 a stained glass window, funded by public subscription, was installed in her memory. It depicts St Augustine of Canterbury (whose name is abbreviated as Austin), St John, the sons of Korah and, at the top, David playing his harp, in true Mary Crawford fashion.

I sat and watched as the feet of dozens of visitors tapped over the tomb. A few paused to pay homage, or simply to give the name of an English novelist a second look, prompted by the guidebook. After a while I got up and went to look at some of the cathedral's other glories, including the serene Epiphany Chapel, suffused with a rainbow glow from its Burne-Jones windows, and the mortuary chests containing the remains of assorted kings of England, among them the Saxons Egbert and Ethelwulf, the Dane Canute, and the extremely unpopular Norman, William Rufus. Outside the entrance to the crypt stood bucketloads of white lilies and eucalyptus, waiting to banish the unadorned days of Lent that were almost at an end.

In the crypt itself there is a modern statue, presented to the cathedral by its sculptor, Antony Gormley. 'Sound II' is designed to stand in water (the crypt regularly floods) and gazes downwards, hands cupped, in a pose of meditation and reflection. The combination of statue and setting, simple as they are, is breathtakingly beautiful.

The gleaming hussars had dispersed by the time I emerged from the cathedral and lunchtime sandwich-eaters had taken their place on the grass in the spring sunshine. I found the City Museum just across the green and popped in to see the few exhibits related to Jane Austen. The museum was hosting an Easter holiday children's trail, and the front desk was littered with colouring sheets and stubs of crayon. Tucked away on the ground floor is a small display case containing two exquisite beaded purses that once belonged to Jane. The smaller is just big enough for a couple of modern pound coins; the larger is made of brightly coloured blue beads, with two cornucopias at the bottom, and is thought to have been worked by Jane herself. There is also an ivory etui or spool case containing a bobbin for winding silks, its top engraved with the ornate initials 'JA'. They are tiny but somehow fitting fragments of a life that, though huge in its influence, was never characterised by possessions.

Also on display was the tiny manuscript of a comic poem that Jane wrote in 1811. It refers to a Miss Beckford of Basing Park in Hampshire and offers yet another reminder of the fun that Jane had at the expense of illness:

> I've a pain in my head
> Said the suffering Beckford
> To her Doctor so dread
> Oh! What shall I take for it?

I stopped off to do a bit of shopping on the way back to the station. The ceremonials over, the off-duty hussars were taking a stroll down the High Street with their families. An attractive girl, her hair loose, her hips swaying in a full-skirt and high-heeled boots, hung proudly onto the arm of an officer whose glinting spurs clinked on the pavement as they walked along. As I browsed among some market stalls I was startled to see a tank rumbling down the road beyond, but no one else seemed to notice.

My return train was also delayed, this time by a broken-down freight train at Micheldever. As the train slowed to a virtual standstill I realized that I was almost back at the place where my journey had begun, deep in the Hampshire countryside close to Steventon. This time, though, I sat above it, cocooned in a 21st-century railway carriage, forced to look down from a viaduct onto the thatched cottages and church spires. Mobile phones trilled around me and there was an apologetic announcement. When there is now so much that separates our world from hers, why are readers across the globe still so in thrall to Jane Austen's work? My journey in her footsteps almost over, I realized that the time had come to try to answer the question.

Afterword
The Pilgrim's Way

*It encourages me... to believe that I have not yet – as
every almost every Writer of Fancy does sooner or later –
overwritten myself.* – Letter to the Countess of Morley,
31 December 1815

At Godmersham Park I went for a walk along the public foot-
path that leads from just inside the gates up onto the downs that
shelter the house on its western side. After climbing steadily for
three quarters of a mile or so, the path joins the North Downs
Way.

For much of its 150-mile length from Farnham to
Canterbury, this long-distance path follows the route of the old
Pilgrim's Way, which connected Winchester and Canterbury,
and was followed by those journeying to the shrine of
Archbishop Thomas Becket, murdered at Canterbury in 1170.
Just above Godmersham the pilgrims caught their first momen-
tous glimpse of their hallowed goal. Almost a thousand years
later, I squinted at Canterbury Cathedral from the same spot as
it shimmered in the summer heat haze five or so miles away.

Chaucer began writing *The Canterbury Tales* some 200 years
after the murder of Thomas Becket, when the pilgrimage was at

the height of its popularity, though for some it had already become more of a leisure pursuit than a form of penance. Indeed there was a growing feeling that the pilgrimage was nothing but an excuse for sinful living along the way. In the 16th century the shrine of the martyred archbishop was destroyed on the orders of Henry VIII and pilgrimages to Canterbury came to an end. Among the relics we are left with are *The Canterbury Tales*, a book still being deciphered by schoolchildren, and the word 'canter', which was originally short for 'Canterbury gallop', the gentle pace at which the pilgrims approached their destination.

Cantering to the end of my own journey in Jane Austen's footsteps, I realised that I had almost followed the old pilgrim's route. I had visited Winchester, Alton, Box Hill and now Godmersham, all places on it or close to it. It made me realize that to follow Jane Austen across southern England is to visit places steeped in centuries of history, places that epitomize the 'green and pleasant land', that rosy view of England still so cherished, here and abroad.

That is one reason why Jane Austen's popularity keeps on growing today. In our uncertain world the places she visited and the books she wrote stand, for many of us, as symbols of the things we most value, the rich history that has made us what we are. Film and television adaptations of her work, and places like Chawton Cottage or the Jane Austen Centre in Bath, fill us with nostalgia for a time when life was simpler and more graceful, a time when tea was always served in china cups on clean tablecloths, women wore pretty dresses and men bowed low. Her 'romances' are marketed in gentle pastel covers to appeal to those who want to cushion themselves within stories of yesteryear that have happy endings.

It's all an illusion, of course. We none of us remember such a time and Jane Austen has come to signify a way of life that she herself would hardly recognize. Her days were not spent arranging flowers or simpering at men in velvet tail coats. She was an acerbic, driven woman, of whom many people were probably wary. She loved a party, but had no trouble being alone, particularly if she had a pen in her hand, and, though she famously never found love, she enjoyed something she prized much higher: the rare thrill (for a woman), if only for a few short years, of seeing her work in print.

In his book *Recreating Jane Austen* John Wiltshire writes: 'Every cultural creation, even a cathedral, has an afterlife, unpredictable, uncontrolled by its original architect, when another era, another cultural configuration turns it, adapts it to its own use.'[1] Wiltshire aims to confront those readers who still consider Jane Austen as a novelist who created a world that is 'far off, impeccably gracious and morally superannuated', who panders to a taste like that of Susan Price in *Mansfield Park* for the "genteel and well appointed"'.

I too wanted to portray Jane Austen as our contemporary in this book. By visiting and describing the places most associated with her, I wanted to demonstrate that, while they have changed, often out of all recognition, Jane Austen still 'works' in our modern world, without all the trappings of nostalgia. She is, as Wiltshire puts it, 'sassy, spunky, post-colonial, radical, transgressive, sexually complex and ambiguous'. Above all, she is still laugh-out-loud funny.

Re-reading Jane Austen's novels is always a joy. Getting to know their author through her letters, then putting her words in a physical context by visiting the places where they were written, was a fascinating experience, which has already added greatly to my enjoyment of her fiction. However trivial their subject matter, the letters frequently leave you open-mouthed in awe at their writer's economy of expression, her acerbic wit and her ability to nail a character in your mind in the fewest of words.

The wonderful Posy Simmonds once drew a cartoon strip in which Jane Austen contemplates journeying into our own times to bask in the worldwide adoration that now surrounds her work. In the first frame a television presenter shouts: 'Jane! Jane! Come on over! The Nation has voted! You are the Number One Pillar of English Lit!... You're a Celebrity... get yourself over here.' Jane almost crosses the 'Stygian divide' to receive the laurels and fanfare that she feels to be her due. Then the prospect of impertinent questions as to the number of her sexual partners, the ecological effects of writing on little bits of ivory and her opinion of Colin Firth's lunchbox convince her to stay in her own time.[2]

In one sense Simmonds is right. Any attempt to drag Jane Austen over to the 21st century is doomed to failure. Our modern sensibilities and interpretations just muddy her genius. This is certainly the view of traditionalists, who prefer to preserve her memory with sprig-muslin dresses and rattling tea-cups. What I discovered on my journey, however, was that embroidering Jane Austen in this way just makes my sense of the real woman fade even further. It was the places that had made little or no attempt to pin down a 'heritage' Jane – Godmersham, Lyme Regis and Steventon – where her words caught light, her characters lived on the page and I felt I knew her just a little.

In these places there was nothing to guide me but her letters and, sometimes, her novels. Jane Austen tea towels and the like are all very well (I have a key ring myself), but her words are the only souvenirs from the journey really worth having.

Acknowledgements

Love and thanks are due to: David, my travelling companion in Hampshire and in life, even though he still can't stand *Mansfield Park*; my mother, whose school prize copy of *Pride and Prejudice* was the start of it; my father, a man with much to recommend him despite the fact he never reads novels; Alexander and Julia: long may you roll down the green slopes. I evol uoy; Christina Stead, not my sister but almost like a Cassandra to me nevertheless; the godfathers: Nick Sumner (you must surely now regret calling Jane Austen 'that prissy tart') and Toby Whitty (I forgive you for standing by Mark Twain's remark that 'any library is a good library that does not contain a volume by Jane Austen, even if it contains no other book'); and Sarah Such, whom it is my great good fortune to call my editor – thank you for your serenity and your dozens of good suggestions.

I would also like to thank John Sunley for giving me permission to visit Godmersham Park and his estate manager, Greg Ellis, for being so generous with his time and taking the trouble to show me around.

And finally, for warm hospitality and comfortable accommodation in Bath and Hampshire, I am grateful to Robert Hornyold-Strickland and Deirdre Green.

Chapter Notes

To avoid the chapter notes becoming too cumbersome, I have not annotated all the quotations from Jane Austen's letters. However the dates I have quoted should make it easy to find their source in Deirdre Le Faye's excellent edition of *Jane Austen's Letters* (OUP, 1997)

Introduction – 'Important Nothings'
1. Claire Tomalin, *Jane Austen: A Life*, p.124
2. Julian Barnes, *Flaubert's Parrot*, p.38

Chapter One – Steventon: 'The cradle of her genius'
1. J.E Austen-Leigh, *A Memoir of Jane Austen and Other Family Recollections*, p.14
2. Claire Tomalin, *Jane Austen: A Life*, p.6
3. *ibid*, pp.6-7
4. David Nokes, *Jane Austen*, p.59
5. Claire Tomalin, *Jane Austen: A Life*, p.25
6. *www.wellwellwell.co.uk*
7. J.E Austen-Leigh, *A Memoir of Jane Austen and Other Family Recollections*, p.32
8. Harry Henshaw, *Historical Notes and Anecdotes*, p.10
9. Deirdre Le Faye *(ed)*, *Jane Austen's Letters*, pp.347-8
10. *ibid* , p.15

11. Claire Tomalin, *Jane Austen: A Life*, p.119

12. *The Times,* Saturday March 18th, 2006

13. J.E Austen-Leigh, *A Memoir of Jane Austen and Other Family Recollections,* p.141

14. Constance Hill, *Jane Austen: Her Homes and Her Friends*, pp.8-10

15. Poem found on a postcard for sale in Steventon church, and printed by permission of The Jane Austen Memorial Trust, Chawton, Hampshire.

16. J.E Austen-Leigh, *A Memoir of Jane Austen and Other Family Recollections,* p.23

17. Harry Henshaw, *Historical Notes and Anecdotes*, p.13

18. *ibid,* p.14

19. Claire Tomalin, *Jane Austen: A Life*, p.124

20. Nigel Nicolson, *Was Jane Austen Happy in Bath?* p.6

21. David Nokes, *Jane Austen*, pp.216-7

22. Deirdre Le Faye, *Jane Austen: The World of Her Novels*, p.57

23. *ibid,* p.57

24. *ibid,* p.61

25. Constance Hill, *Jane Austen: Her Homes and Her Friends*, p.4

26. *ibid,* p.4

27. J.E Austen-Leigh, *A Memoir of Jane Austen and Other Family Recollections,* pp.24-6

28. G.K. Chesterton, *Preface to Love and Freindship and Other Early Works,* p.xiii

Chapter Two – Bath: 'Smoke and confusion'

1. Maggie Lane, *A Charming Place: Bath in the Life and Novels of Jane Austen*, p.41

2. *ibid,* p.23

3. *ibid*, p.32
4. Claire Tomalin, *Jane Austen: A Life*, p.184
5. Constance Hill, *Jane Austen: Her Homes and Her Friends*, pp.122-25
6. Maggie Lane, *A Charming Place: Bath in the Life and Novels of Jane Austen*, p.79
7. Nigel Nicolson, *Was Jane Austen Happy in Bath?* pp.11-12
8. Carol Shields, *Jane Austen*, p.79

Chapter Three – Lyme Regis: 'A strange stranger'
1. John Fowles, *A Short History of Lyme Regis*, p.7
2. Quotation sourced at Philpot Museum, Lyme Regis, of which John Fowles was formerly curator.
3. John Fowles, *A Short History of Lyme Regis*, p.25
4. *ibid*, p.26
5. *ibid*, p.28
6. M Phillips, *Picture of Lyme Regis and Environs*, pp.5-7, pp.10-13
7. Maggie Lane, *Jane Austen and Lyme Regis*, p.25
8. John Fowles, *A Short History of Lyme Regis*, p.10
9. *ibid*, p.12
10. Maggie Lane, *Jane Austen and Lyme Regis*, pp.50-2
11. Nigel Nicolson, *The World of Jane Austen*, p.128
12. Maggie Lane, *Jane Austen and Lyme Regis*, p.49
13. Constance Hill, *Jane Austen: Her Homes and Her Friends*, p.137
14. John Fowles, *The French Lieutenant's Woman*, p.136
15. Maggie Lane, *Jane Austen and Lyme Regis*, p.16
16. *ibid*, p.14
17. *ibid*, pp.15-16
18. J.E. Austen-Leigh, *A Memoir of Jane Austen and Other Family Recollections*, p.188

19. Claire Tomalin, *Jane Austen: A Life*, p.181

20. John Fowles, *A Short History of Lyme Regis*, p.41

21. *Daily Mail*, Monday January 16th, 2006

22. *The Guardian*, Wednesday January 25th, 2006

23. John Fowles, *The French Lieutenant's Woman*, p.111

24. Constance Hill, *Jane Austen: Her Homes and Her Friends*, p.143

25. Maggie Lane, *Jane Austen and Lyme Regis*, p.35

26. Beatrix Potter, *The Tale of Little Pig Robinson*, p.45

27. Carol Shields, *Jane Austen*, p.160

Chapter Four – Godmersham: 'The only place for happiness'

1. Maggie Lane, *Jane Austen and Names*, pp.11-12

2. Constance Hill, *Jane Austen: Her Homes and Her Friends*, p.198 (facing)

3. Deirdre Le Faye (*ed*), *Jane Austen's Letters*, p.346

4. J.E Austen-Leigh, *A Memoir of Jane Austen and Other Family Recollections*, p.158

5. Claire Tomalin, *Jane Austen: A Life*, pp.136-7

6. Constance Hill, *Jane Austen: Her Homes and Her Friends*, p.202

7. David Nokes, *Jane Austen*, p.395

8. www.bodkin-house-hotel.co.uk

Chapter Five – Chawton: 'Home-made'

1. www.janeausten.co.uk

2. J.E Austen-Leigh, *A Memoir of Jane Austen and Other Family Recollections*, p.90

3. Maggie Lane & David Selwyn (*eds*), *Jane Austen: A Celebration*, p.71

4. J.E Austen-Leigh, *A Memoir of Jane Austen and Other Family Recollections*, p.82

5. Deirdre Le Faye, *Jane Austen: The World of Her Novels*, p.154

6. Claire Tomalin, *Jane Austen: A Life*, p.255

7. Maggie Lane & David Selwyn (*eds*), *Jane Austen: A Celebration*, p.84

8. *ibid*, p.29

9. *ibid*, p.55

10. *ibid*, p.17

11. *J.E Austen-Leigh, A Memoir of Jane Austen and Other Family Recollections*, p.177

12. *ibid*, p.168

13. *ibid*, p.77

14. *ibid*, p.125

15. *ibid*, p.138

16. *ibid*, pp.178-9

17. *Elizabeth Proudman, The Essential Guide to Finding Jane Austen in Chawton*, p.3

18. Claire Tomalin, *Jane Austen: A Life*, p.286

Chapter Six – London and Surrey: 'Dissipation and vice'

1. Constance Hill, *Jane Austen: Her Homes and Her Friends*, p.206

2. Carol Shields, *Jane Austen*, p.7

3. Anne-Marie Edwards, *In the Steps of Jane Austen*, p.174

4. Sarah Jane Forder, *Box Hill*, p.3

5. Claire Tomalin, *Jane Austen: A Life*, p.252

Chapter Seven – Winchester: 'July in showers'

1. Jane Austen, *Catharine and Other Writings*, p.246

2. Claire Tomalin, *Jane Austen: A Life*, p.35

3. *ibid*, pp.43-4

4. J.E. Austen-Leigh, *A Memoir of Jane Austen and Other Family Recollections*, p.147

5. Deirdre Le Faye (*ed*), *Jane Austen's Letters*, p.344

6. www.adshg.org.uk

7. Claire Tomalin, *Jane Austen: A Life*, pp.289-90

8. Deirdre Le Faye (*ed*), *The Letters of Jane Austen*, p.347

9. Deirdre Le Faye, *Jane Austen: The World of Her Novels*, p.79

Afterword: The Pilgrim's Way

1. John Wiltshire, *Recreating Jane Austen*, pp.3-9

2. Posy Simmonds, *Literary Life*, p.45

Bibliographical note

I have a large collection of Jane Austen's novels in different editions, including Penguins, Oxford Classics and musty hardbacks bought at second-hand shops. My favourite is a yellowing Penguin omnibus edition of the novels, to which I am very attached despite its ghastly pink cover adorned with rosebuds. After suffering several house moves and quite a few Mediterranean beach holidays it is falling apart, but I can't bear to part with it. It was this edition that I carted with me on my journey. However, I have also listed here those editions in which I have found the introductions and notes useful.

The definitive edition of letters is *Jane Austen's Letters*, collected and edited by Deirdre Le Faye (third edition, Oxford University Press, 1997). Meticulously annotated and full of fascinating background information, this marvellous book has been at my side throughout, and will probably remain on my bedside table for years to come. It's a book that anyone interested in Jane Austen should treat themselves to. I have bowed to its scholarship at every stage of writing *A Rambling Fancy*, and found its biographical and topographical indexes completely invaluable, but it's also great to dip into.

There are a vast number of books about Jane Austen. You could easily spend the rest of your life reading about her. I tried not to be daunted and picked out a few books, not quite at random, but almost. Among the many biographies that are available, I owe a particular debt to Claire Tomalin's meticulously researched life of Jane Austen. I also gained a great deal from reading David Nokes' imaginative and thought-provoking version of her life story.

Bibliography

Novels and Letters of Jane Austen

The Penguin Complete Novels of Jane Austen (Penguin, 1983)

Love and Freindship and Other Early Works, G.K. Chesterton (*intro*) (Chatto & Windus, 1929)

Catherine and Other Writings, Margaret Anne Doody (*ed and intro*) (Oxford University Press, 1993)

Lady Susan/The Watsons/Sanditon, Margaret Drabble (*ed and intro*) (Penguin, 1974)

Sense and Sensibility [1811], James Kinsley and Claire Lamont (*eds*) (Oxford University Press, 1970)

Pride and Prejudice [1813], James Kinsley (*ed*), Isobel Armstrong (*intro*) and Frank W. Bradbrook (*notes*) (Oxford University Press, 1990)

Emma [1816], Ronald Blythe (*ed and intro*) (Penguin, 1966)

Northanger Abbey [1817], Anne Henry Ehrenpreis (*ed and intro*) (Penguin, 1972)

Persuasion [1817], John Davie (*ed*) and Claude Rawson (*intro*) (Oxford University Press, 1990)

Jane Austen's Letters (*ed* Deirdre Le Faye) (third edition, Oxford University Press, 1997)

About Jane Austen and her Works

J.E. Austen-Leigh, *A Memoir of Jane Austen and Other Family Recollections* (Oxford University Press, 2002)

Sue Birtwhistle and Susie Conklin, *The Making of Pride and Prejudice* (BBC/Penguin, 1995)

Frederick Bussby, *Jane Austen in Winchester* (Friends of Winchester Cathedral, 1991)

David Cecil, *A Portrait of Jane Austen* (Penguin, 1980)

Anne-Marie Edwards, *In the Steps of Jane Austen* (Countryside Books, 2002)

Dominique Enright, *The Wicked Wit of Jane Austen* (Michael O'Mara, 2002)

E.L. Green-Armytage, *A Map of Bath in the Time of Jane Austen*

Constance Hill, *Jane Austen: Her Homes and Her Friends* (John Lane, 1902)

Jane Austen Centre, Bath, *Exhibition Guide*

Jane Austen's Winchester (Winchester City Council, 1998)

Maggie Lane, *A Charming Place: Bath in the Life and Novels of Jane Austen* (Millstream Books, 1993)

Maggie Lane, *Jane Austen and Names* (Blaise Books, 2002)

Maggie Lane, *Jane Austen and Lyme Regis* (Jane Austen Society, 2003)

Maggie Lane and David Selwyn (*eds*), *Jane Austen: A Celebration* (Carcanet, 2000)

Marghanita Laski, *Jane Austen* (Thames & Hudson, 1997)

Deirdre Le Faye, *Jane Austen: The World of Her Novels* (Frances Lincoln, 2003)

Nigel Nicolson, *The World of Jane Austen* (Weidenfeld & Nicolson, 1995)

Nigel Nicolson, *Godmersham Park, Kent: Before, During and After Jane Austen's Time* (Jane Austen Society, 1996)

Nigel Nicolson, *Was Jane Austen Happy in Bath?* (Bath: Holburne Museum of Art, 2002)

David Nokes, *Jane Austen: A Life* (Fourth Estate, 1997)

Kate Paul and Rosemary Harden, *Jane Austen: Film and Fashion* (Bath: Assembly Rooms and Museum of Costume, 2004)

Elizabeth Proudman, *The Essential Guide to Finding Jane Austen in Chawton* (Jane Austen Society of North America, 2003)

Carol Shields, *Jane Austen* (Phoenix, 2001)

The Short Guide to Jane Austen's House (Jarrold Publishing and Jane Austen Memorial Trust, 2004)

Olivia Thompson, *How to Win the Mating Game!* (Jarrold Publishing and Jane Austen Memorial Trust, 2005)

Claire Tomalin, *Jane Austen: A Life* (Penguin, 2000)

Sylvia Townsend Warner, *Jane Austen* (British Council and National Book League, 1951)

John Wiltshire, *Recreating Jane Austen* (Cambridge University Press, 2001)

Other Works Consulted

Julian Barnes, *Flaubert's Parrot* (Picador, 1985)

Nigel J. Clarke, *The Book of the Cobb* (Cobblyme Publications, 2003)

Antonia Cunningham, *Winchester Cathedral: A Short Tour* (Scala, 2006)

Charles Dickens, *The Pickwick Papers* [1836–37], (Everyman's Library, 1965)

Dorothy Eagle and Hilary Carnell, *The Oxford Illustrated Literary Guide to*

Great Britain and Ireland (Oxford University Press/Spring Books, 1987)

Helen Fielding, *Bridget Jones's Diary* (Picador, 1996)

Sarah Jane Forder, *Box Hill* (National Trust, 1997)

John Fowles, *The French Lieutenant's Woman* [1969] (Triad Panther, 1977)

John Fowles, *A Short History of Lyme Regis* (Dovecote Press, 1991)

David Gadd, *Georgian Summer: Bath in the Eighteenth Century* (Adams & Dart, 1971)

Godmersham Park: A Short History

Harry Henshaw, *Historical Notes and Anecdotes* [written c. 1949] (Rector and Churchwarden of St Nicholas Church, Steventon, Hampshire, 1997; Members of the Congregation, Church of St Nicholas, Steventon, Hampshire, Steventon PCC 2003)

Alison Kelly, *Mrs Coade's Stone* (Self-Publishing Association, 1990)

Hermione Lee, *Body Parts: Essays on Life Writing* (Chatto & Windus, 2005)

M. Phillips, *Picture of Lyme Regis and Environs* (Tucker & Toms, 1817)

J.H. Plumb, *The First Four Georges* (Collins Fontana, 1975)

Beatrix Potter, *The Tale of Little Pig Robinson* (Frederick Warne, 1930)

Hugh Schryver, *The Parish Church of St Lawrence the Martyr, Godmersham, Kent: A Souvenir Guide*

George Bernard Shaw, *Pygmalion* (film version) (Penguin, 1941)

Posy Simmonds, *Literary Life* (Jonathan Cape, 2003)

Edward Thomas, *Selected Poems* (Faber, 1977)

Andrea Wulf and Emma Gieben-Gamal, *This Other Eden: Seven Great Gardens and Three Hundred Years of English History* (Little, Brown, 2005)

Tony White

Another Fool in the Balkans

in the footsteps of
Rebecca West

Michael Montgomery

Lear's Italy

in the footsteps of
Edward Lear

Well travelled...
well read.

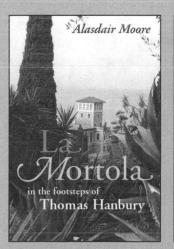

Alasdair Moore

La Mortola

in the footsteps of
Thomas Hanbury

Mathew Lyons

There and Back Again

in the footsteps of
J.R.R. Tolkien

Available from all good bookshops
www.cadoganguides.com

CADOGAN